Pocket Book of the Gern

NAVAL & MILITARY PRESS

ISBN 1843424045

1

DISTRIBUTION

Lieut-Colonels' Commands   ...   Scale A + 1 for each I O

CONTENTS

PART II.—ORGANIZATION

4

CHAPTER 2.—AIRBORNE TROOPS AND GAF
TRANSPORT

INTRODUCTION

This " Pocket Book of the German Army " is intended for the use of intelligence officers of field formations and units.

Intelligence officers have in " The German Forces in the Field," " Order of Battle of the German Army," and " Guide to the Identification of German Units," works of reference which can be carried in the field, and which should enable them to answer their commander's questions on the subjects with which these publications deal.

On points of organization and equipment intelligence officers have hitherto had either to trust to memory, or carry with them " Notes on the German Army—War," " New Notes on the German Army Nos. 1—4," and, in addition, a quantity of papers amending these publications which are circulated through " I " channels and for the most part in roneod form. This Pocket Book is intended to meet the obvious need for a work of reference on the organization and equipment of the German Army.

This Pocket Book supersedes " New Notes on the German Army : No. 1—Armoured and Motorized Divisions, 1942." In consequence of its publication, " Notes on the German Army—War, 1940," and " New Notes on the German Army, Nos. 2 and 3," will be withdrawn from all holders below divisional HQ. HQ retaining these three publications for reference should treat this Pocket Book as superseding them where they are at variance with it. Where more detailed information is required than can be given in this Pocket Book, the earlier publications may still be of use, though holders will have to exercise discretion in deciding whether to rely on the earlier publications or apply to higher authority for guidance. The " New Notes on the German Army " series is for the time being suspended, though it may be continued, if it is found that there is a demand for it after the issue of this Pocket Book.

Part I of the Pocket Book on the general principles of German army organization and tactics is intended to supply the background necessary for a proper understanding of the highly summarized tables in the remainder of the book. It must, however, be emphasized that this Pocket Book does not purport to be anything more than an *aide memoire* for intelligence officers and that its publication does not absolve intelligence officers from the study of Intelligence Summaries and other papers circulated through " I " channels, which will provide the more detailed background of information

As a work of reference, however, this Pocket Book will be kept up to date by the issue of printed amendments.

Suggested methods of using this Pocket Book in the field will be found in the preface to Part II.

Finally, since this Pocket Book is intended to be a work of practical utility, suggestions for its improvement will be welcomed, particularly from officers who have used it on exercises or in the field. Suggestions should be addressed to the Director of Military Intelligence (M I 14), War Office.

PART I

GENERAL PRINCIPLES OF GERMAN ORGANIZATION AND TACTICS

CHAPTER 1

TYPES OF DIVISIONS

Section 1.—INFANTRY DIVISIONS— ORGANIZATION

1. **General.**—Infantry divisions, which form the great bulk of the German army, are still organized on a horse-drawn basis. The only divisional unit that is mechanized throughout is the anti-tank battalion. All other units include only a limited number of mechanized vehicles ; most of the personnel march and a great part of the equipment is carried on horse-drawn vehicles.

2. **Infantry regiment.**—German infantry regiments, of which there are three in the division, correspond approximately to a British brigade group. The regiment consists of three battalions, a mounted infantry (or cyclist) platoon, an infantry pioneer platoon,* an anti-tank company, and an infantry gun company, which includes guns of 15-cm (5·91-in) calibre. The inclusion of the infantry gun company is a good example of the German principle of decentralizing heavy weapons. Instead of keeping all their artillery under divisional control, the Germans place that part of it which is specially designed for close support under the control of the commander of the infantry regiment. Each battalion consists of three rifle companies and a MG company equipped with medium MGs.

3. **Artillery regiment.**—The artillery regiment consists of three field batteries and one medium battery, with a total of 36 × 10·5-cm (4·14-in) gun-howitzers and twelve medium equipments (10·5-cm (4·14-in) guns and 15-cm (5·91-in) howitzers). The number of barrels in the German divisional artillery regiment is thus considerably smaller than that in

---

* Infantry pioneers are infantry personnel trained in minor engineer duties, and also in assault operations against fixed defences and strong points.

a British artillery regiment, but two factors must be borne in mind :—

    (a) German artillery fires heavier projectiles than the British. Thus the 10.5-cm (4.14-in) gun-howitzer, the equivalent of the British 25-pr, fires a 32-lb projectile ;

    (b) German infantry regiments include weapons which we would class as artillery.

    4. Reconnaissance unit.—Reconnaissance units in a German infantry division are quite different from any in the British army. The normal reconnaissance unit consists of a horsed (sabre) squadron, a cyclist squadron, and a mechanized heavy squadron which includes armoured cars, infantry (close support) guns, anti-tank guns, and mortars.

    5. Engineer battalion.—The engineer battalion includes three companies, of which only one is fully mechanized, and in addition a bridging column capable of taking the 22-ton Pz Kw IV tank.

    6. Anti-tank battalion.—The anti-tank battalion, which is mechanized throughout, includes 27 5-cm (1.97-in) or 7.5-cm (2.95-in) guns. It must, however, be remembered that each infantry regiment also includes anti-tank guns.

SECTION 2.—INFANTRY DIVISIONS—TACTICS

    1. Attack.—The German infantry in the attack employs tactics very similar to our own. Within the section, tactics are based on covering fire from the LMG, which has a detachment of three men, of whom the No. 3 serves entirely as an ammunition number. Medium machine guns, although organized separately in the fourth company of each battalion, are normally attached by platoons to the rifle companies and give covering fire to the infantry as they advance, moving forward from cover to cover by bounds ; they are trained to change position rapidly if engaged. Mortars are very skilfully used ; the weapon is no different in performance from our own but always in the past it has been imaginatively and skilfully handled ; it has been found that many mortar positions are sited on reverse slopes to cover the forward slopes ; seldom are more than a few rounds fired from any one position even if the mortar's position has not been engaged by enemy fire.

In German training particular emphasis is placed on infiltration tactics round flanks and between individual defensive positions to encircle and squeeze out those positions singly.

The infantry guns—7·5-cm (2·95-in) and 15-cm (5·91-in)—
are normally employed well forward, though the heavier ones
may be held by the regimental commander in the area of
regimental (= British brigade) HQ. They are employed to
thicken the covering fire for troops advancing.

2. **Defence.**—The two cardinal principles of German
defensive practice are :—

    (a) to destroy the oncoming enemy by a progressively
        increasing weight of fire before he reaches the
        FDLs, and

    (b) counter-attack, both immediate and prepared—a
        counter-attack is almost invariable ; it is determined,
        and as heavy as available strength permits.

German infantry defence follows, at least in theory,
a system which is more detailed than our own. The
German defensive position consists, first of all, of
" advanced positions " (for which there are no equivalents
in our own static practice), whose purpose is to provide a
light delaying screen 5,000-7,000 yds forward of the FDLs
but still within range of divisional artillery, and to cause
the enemy to deploy at the earliest moment. In rear of this,
usually some 2,000 yds forward of the FDLs, and within
range of all divisional artillery, including infantry guns and
possibly mortars, come the " battle outposts," which correspond roughly with our own outpost line. Those are normally
found from the troops manning the FDLs and will attempt
to hold up the attack as long as possible. They will probably
be quite strong. The main position in the " main battle
zone " consists of a mesh of strong points, which are called
by the Germans " nests of all arms." These are sited, where
ground permits, on commanding features, making very
skilful use of ground. Where the ground between the strong
points cannot be covered by fire from adjacent strong points,
this ground will be protected by wire or mines or anti-tank
ditches, or by any combination of two or more of these.
These obstacles are intended to canalize the attack and to
force it to run into the fire of the defenders at their main
concentration of infantry or anti-tank weapons. Emphasis is
laid on skilful and extensive sniping.

3. **Coastal defence.**—Here, the edge of the coast is the
forward edge of the main battle zone, so that the attempt
is made to prepare the destruction of the enemy forward of
the FDLs by the use of heavy coastal artillery, medium and
field artillery, and anti-tank artillery, enfilading the shore,
etc. The coast itself is fortified extensively both with and
without concrete, etc. The mobile reserves for prepared

counter-attack are situated some 20-30 miles from the coast line and consist of armoured and motorized divisions.

4. Withdrawal.—Here, again, the German practice largely corresponds with our own. The most rearward infantry element left confronting the enemy will probably be lorry-borne. The Germans leave a strong artillery, A tk, and AA A tk screen to the last, with their rearguards. The German engineers carry out extensive and very thorough demolitions, also leaving a large number of clever booby traps.

Section 3.—MOTORIZED DIVISIONS— ORGANIZATION

1. Motorized divisions are organized for close co-operation with armoured divisions and are (as their name implies) mechanized throughout.

2. A motorized division differs from an infantry division in four main respects :—

    (a) A motorized division includes a tank battalion.

    (b) A motorized division includes only two infantry regiments.

    (c) The artillery regiment in a motorized division has only two field batteries, a medium battery, and an AA battery.

    (d) The reconnaissance element in a motorized division is provided by an armoured reconnaissance unit consisting of an armoured car squadron, three armoured reconnaissance companies (transported either in armoured carriers or " Volkswagen " or on MC), and a heavy company.

3. An infantry regiment in a motorized division (like an infantry regiment in a normal infantry division) includes close-support and anti-tank guns in accordance with the German principle of decentralizing heavy weapons.

Section 4.—MOTORIZED DIVISIONS—TACTICS

The tactics of German motorized divisions are now probably similar to those of our composite divisions. Formerly they were used as ordinary infantry to take over ground from the Panzer Grenadiers (infantry) of the armoured division and also to reinforce a prepared attack by the latter. It is presumed that they will retain this role, but the inclusion of a tank battalion in them will enable them to take on increasingly independent roles.

SECTION 5.—ARMOURED DIVISIONS— ORGANIZATION

1. **General.**—The German armoured division consists of a tank regiment, a Panzer Grenadier (infantry) brigade, and supporting units, which come directly under divisional headquarters.

2. **Tank regiment.**—The German tank regiment normally consists of three battalions with a total of 164 tanks. It includes two types of fighting tanks, the 22-ton Pz Kw III and IV, and also the 9-ton Pz Kw II at regimental and battalion headquarters for liaison and reconnaissance. The re-equipment of the tank regiment with a new medium tank (known as the Panther) and the new 56-ton Pz Kw VI (or Tiger) tank is to be expected in the near future.

3. **Panzer Grenadier brigade.**—The Panzer Grenadier brigade consists of two Panzer Grenadier regiments. These regiments possess great fire-power, for they include infantry and anti-tank guns. Rifle companies in Panzer Grenadier regiments equipped with armoured troop carrying vehicles are called by the Germans " armoured " rifle companies to distinguish them from the " mechanized " companies carried in lorries. The allotment of armoured companies is not fixed. For the sake of example, the brigade shown at Table 21 has one armoured and one mechanized regiment. It is however possible to have one armoured and one mechanized battalion in the same regiment, or battalions with one armoured and two mechanized companies or any other variation. This is a good example of the flexibility of German organization. The main point of interest in the organization of armoured (as distinct from the mechanized) rifle companies is the allocation of anti-tank guns to platoons.

4. **Reconnaissance.**—The armoured reconnaissance unit in the armoured division (like that in the motorized division) consists of an armoured car squadron (with 24 armoured cars), three armoured reconnaissance companies (transported either in armoured carriers or " Volkswagen " or on MC), and a heavy company, which includes anti-tank guns, close support guns, and a pioneer platoon.

5. **Artillery regiment.**—The artillery regiment (like that in the motorized division) consists of two field batteries, a medium battery, and an AA battery.

6. **Engineer battalion.**—The engineer battalion (like that in the infantry division) consists of three companies and a bridging column. It is, however, mechanized throughout, and one of the three companies is an armoured engineer company equipped with armoured troop carrying vehicles.

7. Anti-tank battalion.—The anti-tank battalion is organized in the same way as the anti-tank battalion in an infantry or motorized division with twenty seven 5-cm (1·97-in) or 7·5-cm (2·95-in) anti-tank guns. There are also anti-tank guns in other units of the armoured division.

Section 6.—ARMOURED DIVISIONS—TACTICS

1. **Attack.**—The thrusting tactics of the German armoured division are notorious. It is their ultimate mission to break through the enemy lines and to disrupt communications and rear areas. In the Battle of France this was carried out by battle groups moving more or less independently along the roads ; in North Africa, battle formations were less road bound and battle groups tended to move in fairly compact mobile defended localities in the form of a moving mass. It is probable that under European conditions German tanks will revert to longer and narrower formations, but they will still, as before, when making a prepared attack, launch it in waves, in which the most normal method is as follows :—

The first wave thrusts to the enemy's artillery. The second wave gives covering fire to the first wave, then attacks the enemy infantry zone preceded, accompanied, or followed, by the Panzer Grenadiers, which debus at the last possible moment ; the tanks' objectives are the enemy anti-tank defences and infantry positions, which will be attacked with HE and MG fire, the tank's gun serving not so much as its major offensive weapon (which is the MG at this stage) as its own anti-tank protection. The third wave mops up, with the next wave of Panzer Grenadiers. Some armoured divisions are strong in SP artillery, which moves very far forward in battle groups and engages likely targets over open sights, normally at ranges of 1,000 yds and below. They are also strong in anti-tank guns, frequently including SP; these are intended to perform the same functions as destroyers in relation to battleships in protecting the tanks by neutralizing the fire of the enemy's anti-tank artillery.

2. **Defence.**—In defence the armoured division is used as a counter-attack reserve. Here also it is likely that it will be employed in battle groups, of which a likely tactic is for infantry to pin down the attacker frontally, while the tanks work round one or both flanks to pinch out the enemy salient.

Section 7.—MOUNTAIN DIVISIONS— ORGANIZATION

1. **General.**—The mountain division differs from the infantry division in the following main respects :—

(a) The mountain division has two infantry regiments in place of three.

(b) The principle of decentralizing heavy weapons is carried a step further in the mountain infantry than in the normal infantry regiment. There is no infantry gun company in the mountain infantry regiment, but close support weapons are put into a fifth company in each battalion, thus enabling the battalion to operate independently, as is frequently necessary in mountainous country.

(c) The normal divisional artillery regiment is replaced in the mountain division by a mountain artillery regiment of three batteries of 7·5-cm (2·95-in) mountain guns and one battery of heavier weapons.

2. **Anti-tank battalion.**—The anti-tank battalion in the mountain division is organized in the same way as the anti-tank battalion of the infantry, motorized, or armoured divisions. This is an example of another important principle in German army organization—the standardization of units throughout various types of division. Other examples have been mentioned in the course of this chapter. The artillery regiment and the armoured reconnaissance unit in an armoured division, for example, are organized in the same way as those in the motorized division. The standardization of units greatly simplifies all problems of training, equipment, maintenance, and supply.

3. **Allotment of weapons.**—Mountain divisions are flexibly organized for employment in various types of terrain, and the allotment of weapons to the division will vary to some extent according to the type of country in which the division is operating. The mountain artillery regiment may for example be reinforced or replaced by an artillery regiment equipped with field and medium equipments.

4. **Transport.**—The mountain division has a certain number of mechanized units, *e.g.*, the anti-tank battalion and the heavy company of the recce unit. The other units are for the most part dependent on pack and horse-drawn transport, the proportions of each type allotted depending on the type of country in which the division is operating. Mountain carrier battalions or companies may also be allotted to divisional supply services, when the division is operating in country where loads have to be man-handled.

Section 8.—MOUNTAIN DIVISIONS—TACTICS

German mountain divisions have been characterized by the same spirit of boldness and thrust as the armoured divisions. They include expert Tyrolean and Bavarian mountaineers. The mountain divisions split up in mountainous country into small independent battle groups which infiltrate into and soften up the enemy positions. Little is known of the actual minor tactics employed by the mountain troops.

SECTION 9.—LIGHT DIVISIONS— ORGANIZATION

1. It is as yet possible to give only a tentative organization for light divisions. It appears, however, that they are of two types—the first, referred to in this Pocket Book for convenience as Type " A," which is organized on a mechanized basis, and a second referred to as Type " B," which is organized on a horse-drawn basis.

2. **Type " A "—mechanized.**—This type consists of :—

> Two infantry regiments, organized on the same lines as the infantry regiments in a motorized division.
> Artillery regiment, of two field batteries and one medium battery.
> Other divisional units (anti-tank, engineer, signals, reconnaissance).

It is believed that in this type of division the artillery regiment and other divisional units are mechanized throughout, while the personnel of the infantry regiments are transported by troop-carrying MT regiments from the GHQ Pool.

3. **Type " B "—horse-drawn.**—This type of division consists of :—

> Two infantry regiments, organized on the same lines as the infantry regiments in the mountain division.
> Artillery regiment, of two field batteries and one medium battery.
> Other divisional units (anti-tank, engineer, signals, reconnaissance).

This type of division is clearly intended to be available, when required, for mountain warfare. The allotment of weapons (e.g., to the artillery regiment) and of pack and horse-drawn transport will therefore vary with the type of country over which the division is operating.

SECTION 10.—LIGHT DIVISIONS—TACTICS

The tactics of the light division (irrespective of its exact organization) will probably not vary fundamentally from those of the motorized and mountain divisions.

CHAPTER 2

GHQ TROOPS

Section 11.—GENERAL

1. In the German field army specialist non-divisional units of all types are grouped together in the GHQ pool, from which they are allotted to army groups and armies, and sub-allotted, if necessary, to corps and divisions.

2. In this Pocket Book it is possible to set out the organization of only the more important combatant units in the GHQ pool. The functions of some of these units (*e.g.*, MG battalions) will be apparent from the organizational tables given in Part II. Brief notes are appended on other GHQ units.

Section 12.—AA UNITS

1. AA defence is in the main the responsibility of the German air force, and GAF AA units will be found operating with the field army (*see* Part III).

2. The GHQ pool, however, includes the following *army* AA units :—*

    (*a*) Motorized AA battalions (*Fla-Bataillon*), which form part of the infantry arm.

    (*b*) AA batteries (*Heeresflak*), which form part of the artillery arm.

Section 13.—SMOKE AND CHEMICAL WARFARE TROOPS

1. **General.**—The primary role (to which the Germans attach great importance) of the smoke troops is, as their name implies, the putting down of smoke screens. Smoke units are frequently allotted to corps, and in any large scale operation, smoke will be fired by smoke troops and artillery together under the control of the artillery commander.

In the event, however, of chemical warfare breaking out, the smoke troops would, in co-operation with other arms, play a part in offensive chemical warfare, for which their equipment is well suited. Brief notes are appended on the potential functions of the various arms of the service in

---

  * Certain army units also include AA elements, *e.g.* :—

    (i) AA (*Fla*) companies in tank regiments and A tk battalions (*see* Tables 20 and 22).

    (ii) AA (*Heeresflak*) batteries in the divisional artillery regiment of armoured and motorized divisions (*see* pages 62 and 52).

chemical warfare in order to bring the role of the smoke troops into perspective.

2. **Offensive chemical warfare.**—German *infantry* can fire tear gas projectiles from their mortars and 7·5-cm (2·95-in) infantry guns and lethal gas from their 15-cm (5·91-in) infantry guns. In addition, a heavy projector on the rocket principle (the primary role of which is to attack area targets with HE and incendiary projectiles, but which could also be used for putting down a concentration of gas) is being issued to Panzer Grenadier regiments in armoured divisions.

Both the 10·5-cm (4·14-in) gun howitzers and the 15-cm (5·91-in) medium howitzers of divisional *artillery* regiments can fire all types of gas chargings. It is known also that the divisional artillery regiments of the " Grossdeutschland " division and probably twenty infantry divisions formed since December, 1941, include a smoke troop equipped with 15-cm (5·91-in) smoke mortars 41, constructed on the rocket principle, for which gas-charged ammunition is available.

Armoured *engineer* companies in armoured divisions are to be issued with heavy projectors. Blister gas will, in the event of chemical warfare breaking out, be issued to infantry pioneer platoons, mechanized pioneer platoons, and engineer units, to enable them to contaminate the neighbourhood of road-blocks, etc., in order to make them more effective obstacles.

Smoke units suitable for offensive chemical warfare include the following types :—

    (a) Smoke regiments, equipped with 10·5-cm (4·14-in) smoke mortars.

    (b) Heavy smoke regiments, equipped with 15-cm (5·91-in) (or heavier) smoke mortars and heavy projectors on the rocket principle.

    (c) Decontamination batteries (which can be converted to contamination batteries at short notice).

N.B.—In any assessment of the Germans' offensive CW potential in a given theatre, the availability of aircraft should not be overlooked, since the Germans appear to be attaching increasing importance to the use of aircraft spray and gas bombs.

3. **Defensive chemical warfare.**—The Germans have a high and possibly exaggerated opinion of the value of mustard gas as a means of imposing delay. As a corollary, they regard ground contamination as a serious menace to the movement of their own troops and have equipped and trained themselves elaborately to meet this threat.

All troops are equipped on an adequate scale with standard materials for personal and weapon decontamination. Infantry pioneer platoons, mechanized pioneer platoons, and engineer companies, are equipped with decontamination powder. The gas scout sections formed by companies and equivalent sub-units are equipped with light anti-gas clothing, and have the duty of reconnoitring and marking off contaminated areas. All motorized troops, whose vehicles can be readily adapted for the purpose, are intended to be trained in ground decontamination.

Smoke troops include specialist decontamination units of the following types :—

(a) Decontamination batteries.

(b) Road decontamination batteries.

CHAPTER 3

SUPPLY AND ADMINISTRATIVE SERVICES

Section 14.—INTRODUCTION

1. It has been decided to devote a considerable amount of space in this Pocket Book to a summary of the German supply and administrative services, since it has been found that a working knowledge of the system is essential for intelligence officers at higher formation HQ in the field. More detailed information will be found in " New Notes on the German Army, No. 4."

2. German supply and administrative services are characterized by adaptability and flexibility. Administration is simple in that spheres of responsibility are few and clearly defined, full use is made of local resources, and the whole organization is capable of the most rapid expansion or contraction in accordance with the military situation.

Section 15.—SUPPLY SERVICES, RATIONS, AMMU- NITION, AND PETROL

1. **Personnel.**—Before considering the detailed organization of the system of supply, a brief description is given below of the various officers, officials, and senior NCOs, who are concerned in maintaining this system of supply at all levels. The list is by no means comprehensive owing to the numbers involved, nor will all the personnel described as being part of a regiment or battalion always be found there. The large part played by officials (Wehrmacht-Beamten) makes it necessary to give a brief account of them.

2. **Officials** are administrative and technical personnel within the armed forces and on the establishment of units. As at present constituted, they are not regarded as " civilians in uniform," and are claimed by the Germans as combatants ; but they form a sort of separate corps within the armed forces, with separate conditions of service and training, and are promoted only inside the corps. They must, however, receive some infantry training. They wear the normal field uniform, with dark green as their distinguishing colour, and a secondary colour to show the branch to which they belong. They may rank either as officers or as other ranks, but the vast majority of officials in forward areas rank as officers.

3. Regiment and unit personnel

(a) *Paymasters (Zahlmeister)*.—Officials at HQ of regiments and units and in many independent companies. They perform roughly the " Q " duties of the staff captain of a British brigade or the duties of a unit QM. They are assisted by a pay clerk (*Rechnungsführer*).

(b) *Messing officers (Verpflegungsoffizier)*.—Officers (occasionally replaced by officials) at HQ of regiments and some battalions in charge of administration of rations. ·

(c) *Messing NCO (Verpflegungsunteroffizier)*.—At regiment HQ he assists the messing officer. There is usually an OR assistant (*Verpflegungsmann*). In units which have no messing officer the messing NCO is responsible to the paymaster.

(d) *NCO storeman (Geräteunteroffizier)*.—He is in charge of the stores and should have done a course at an ammunition depot. He may also have an assistant.

(e) *CSM (Hauptfeldwebel)*.—The senior WO on the strength of a company (including HQ companies). There is not usually a CSM on the establishment of the HQ of regiments or units but practice has varied in this war. Company, squadron, or troop administration is the responsibility of the company commander assisted by the CSM.

4. Personnel at formation HQ

(a) *Second GSO (Ib) (Zweiter Generalstabsoffizier)*.—This officer, who will have been to the Staff College, is the senior officer of the " Q " group of the formation headquarters staff. At corps he is called the *Quartiermeister* and at army *Oberquartiermeister*. He has the general responsibility for all " Q " matters, and has a staff captain to help him (*Zweiter Ordonnanzoffizier*).

(b) *Divisional Supply Officer* (*Kommandeur der Divisions Nachschubtruppen-Kodina*).—Coming directly under control of the second GSO is the supply officer who is not himself on the establishment of formation HQ, but has a staff with a separate organization to control the units under his command which bear the ancillary number of the division. Workshop companies are administratively under command of supply officers, but are operationally under control of the technical officer (*Ingenieur*). (*See Sec 18*, para 1 (*b*).)

(c) *Intendant*.—An official who is entirely responsible for dealing with rations, clothing, and pay. He, with his immediate assistants and clerks, are on the establishment of formation HQ, but the units he commands are separate units (*Verwaltungstruppen*) bearing the divisional ancillary number. (*See Sec 16*, para 4.)

SECTION 16.—ORGANIZATION OF SUPPLY, PETROL, AND AMMUNITION UNITS WITHIN FORMATIONS

The function of *transport* and *handling* of supplies are sharply separated in the German organization.

1. **Transport of supplies, petrol, and ammunition** (*See* diagram para 3.)

(a) *Formation HQ*.—Under the supply officer at formation HQ there are a number of transport columns (*Fahrkolonne*) which undertake the transport of supplies. The number and type of columns vary with the type of formation. They carry all supplies, ammunition, and petrol, and, except for the petrol columns which may be composed of tanker lorries and which carry POL only, are not exclusively concerned with separate commodities. The following columns may be found within a division :—

(i) HT columns (*Fahrkolonne*) of 30 tons capacity in infantry divisions.

(ii) Light HT columns (*Leichte Fahrkolonne*) of 17 tons capacity in some infantry divisions. (Not to be confused with light infantry columns of regiments, etc.)

(iii) Small MT columns (*Kleine Kraftwagen Kolonne*) of 30 tons capacity in nearly all divisions.

(iv) Large MT columns of 60 tons capacity. They may occur in divisions but are mostly non-divisional units.

(v) Small POL columns (*Kleine Kraftwagen-kolonne für Betriebsstoff*) of 5,500 gallons capacity in most infantry divisions.

(vi) Large POL columns of 11,000 gallons capacity in motorized and armoured divisions.

(b) *Division.*—In infantry divisions the degree of mechanization varies greatly. Columns may be :—

(i) Only HT and at most one small POL column (9 HT columns and one small POL).

(ii) Columns half MT and half HT (4 HT and 4 MT).

(iii) Completely MT (8 MT and one small POL).

The second is the most likely to be encountered and the total capacity should be in the region of 250 tons.

In armoured divisions, the columns are far more standardized and entirely mechanized.

(c) *Army.*—At army there are similar columns which perform the same functions.

2. Unit transport

(a) *Light columns (Leichte Infanteriekolonne, Artillerie-kolonne,* etc.) exist. They are primarily for ammunition and are organized as separate sub-units. The following have light columns (either horsed or mechanized and varying considerably in size and strength) :—

Infantry regiments.
Artillery batteries.
Signals battalions.
Engineer battalions.
Reconnaissance units.
Tank battalions.

The anti-tank battalion has no light column, ammunition being carried either with company or battalion transport or in divisional columns.

(b) *Within regiments and battalions* transport is divided up as follows :—

Battle transport (Gefechtstross).—This is the most important part of transport of all companies, battalions, and regimental HQ. It is controlled by the CSM of the company, and usually includes a unit armoury and regimental maintenance personnel (*see Sec 18,* para 1 (*a*) (iii)), a medical NCO, storeman, two cooks, clerks, and drivers ; in mechanized units vehicles include one or more for POL transport.

Baggage transport (*Gepäcktross*).—In companies this is controlled by the pay clerk ; at battalion and regimental HQ it may be commanded by the paymaster, and includes one or more clerks.

Rations transport (*Verpflegungstross*).—At HQ of battalions and regiments the messing officer or messing NCO has one or more vehicles for unit rations transport.

Infantry regiments vary in the extent of mechanization of their unit transport. Battle transport is normally horsed, together with one part of the rations transport. Baggage transport, together with the other part of the rations transport should be mechanized, but is not always so. The organization given above may vary in practice. Battle transport will always be found with the unit, but rations and baggage transport may at any time be placed under regimental control. In Africa this centralization was carried a stage further, light columns and a large part of unit transport being detached for use by divisional and army supply officers.

3. Handling of supplies, petrol, and ammunition.—

The following diagram gives some indication of the spheres of responsibility of the supply officer and of the intendant.

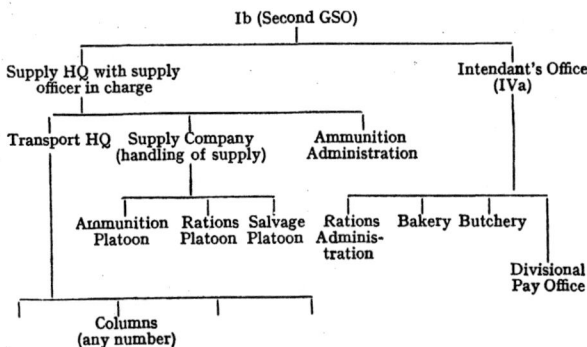

Handling duties are sub-divided into :—

(a) *Labour* done by supply companies.

(b) *Supervision* done by administration and ration platoons.

    (i) *Supply companies* (*Nachschubkompanie*).—The diagram shows that the unit responsible for handling supplies is the supply company, which is controlled by the supply officer (at army there will be supply battalions). These supply companies may be mechanized or partly mechanized, and consist of three platoons, ammunition, rations, and salvage. They are employed on the loading and unloading of columns, the setting up of ammunition points, etc., and various other duties of a similar nature.

(ii) *The supervision* is carried out by an *ammunition* administration platoon and a *rations* administration platoon. Labour and supervision for *petrol* are performed by personnel of the petrol column themselves, supplemented if necessary by a detachment from the divisional supply company. It will be seen that the *rations* administration is not part of the supply company but is under control of the intendant. In practice, therefore, an ammunition (or supply) RP will be formed and worked by ammunition (or rations) personnel of the divisional supply company, supervised by NCOs of the divisional ammunition (or rations) administration.

4. The intendant's section (Intendantur).—The intendant's responsibility includes the administration of rations, clothing, and pay (*Verwaltungsdienst*). Besides this, however, he commands the following :—

(a) Rations administration office (*Verpflegungsamt*). This is a mechanized unit, responsible for divisional rations point and for distribution, returns, etc., of clothing and personal equipment.

(b) Bakery company, horsed or mechanized.

(c) Butcher company, mechanized.

(d) Divisional pay office (*Divisions-Feldkasse*). This consists of one official and one clerk.

5. Non-divisional units.—The supply organization and the responsibilities of the various officers and officials at corps or army are very similar to division. The allotment of supply battalions to an army is normally two, and two supply column battalions, but this allotment naturally varies. In addition there are certain specialist supply companies such as ammunition companies, petrol companies, filling detachments, and on the transport side special independent supply columns such as POL tanker columns, large water columns, mountain carrier battalions (for mountain divisions), which may be allotted for special operations. Special staffs are also allotted to control these units. The whole system is extremely flexible and can be implemented by extra units when necessary.

Section 17.—SYSTEM OF SUPPLY

1. The most important elements in the chain of supply are :—

(a) The *division* in the battle area.

(b) The *army* with its services operating in the L of C area.

(c) The *home area* in which supply is organized by the . head of army supply. (*Ch. H. Rüst. u. B d E.*)

At first corps played little part in the chain of supply and corps columns were used mainly to supplement transport between army and division. Since the war its importance has increased and it is now usual to set up corps rations stores and corps ammunition dumps. A distinction was, however, earlier made between forward army rations stores and main army rations stores ; the change appears to be largely that corps has taken over the forward rations stores, not that a new link has been created between army and division. In general, the system is flexible and simple. Spheres of responsibility are not too many and are clearly defined. Supply authorities are encouraged to send supplies as far forward as possible in the same vehicle without reloading. Since the war there has been a tendency to multiply specialist units, but the organization still remains simple and based on the same principles.

2. Rations.

Responsibility at all levels lies with the intendant.

(a) *Army intendant* is responsible for making full use of the resources of the L of C area. He may indent directly on a base rations office, but probably will indent through GHQ. He sets up a number of army rations stores (*Armee Verpflegungslager*) manned either from the army rations office or supply battalion. A mobile stock of rations may be maintained loaded on trains or army columns.

(b) *Corps intendant* indents on army. He may set up a corps rations store to which rations are brought in corps or army columns.

(c) *Divisional intendant* is responsible for making full use of local resources. What he cannot obtain locally he indents for through corps. He sets up *divisional rations points* to which rations are brought up from army and corps dumps. This **task** may be done directly on army, corps, or divisional columns, or *reloading points (Umschlagstelle)* may be set up by army or corps intendant, from which rations are fetched by divisional columns. Sometimes the railhead may be in the divisional area.

(*d*) Unit rations are brought up by unit rations transport from a divisional rations point. Rations are calculated in *daily issues (Tagessatz)*. Theoretically, one day's issue should be with forward troops and the next on its way. The next eight days' issues are the responsibility of army and should be on their way between army and division.

DIAGRAM OF SUPPLY OF RATIONS

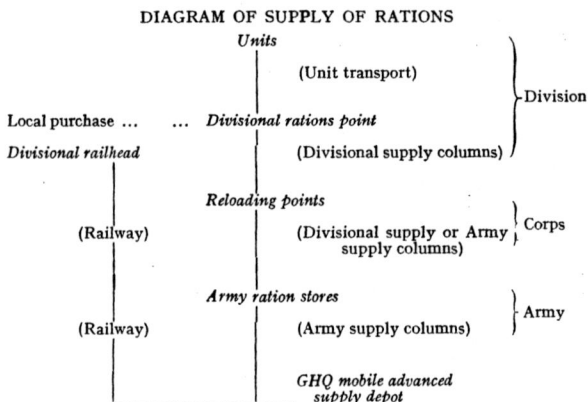

3. **Ammunition**

Responsibility lies with the Second GSO Ib and his technical adviser.

(*a*) Army indents on GHQ. Stocks received are held either in army ammunition depots (*Armee Munitionslager*) set up by the technical adviser who is usually an artillery officer, and manned by the ammunition section of the army supply battalion or as mobile stock in trains or on army columns.

(*b*) Corps indent on army and may set up corps ammunition dumps (*Korps Munitionslager*).

(*c*) Division indents through corps on army. The technical adviser (usually an artillery officer) part of Ib, sets up divisional ammunition points (*Munitions-*

Ausgabestelle). Ammunition is received from army or corps either directly or from army, corps, or divisional columns, or through a *reloading point*. Again divisional railhead may be in the divisional area.

(d) Units collect ammunition in *light columns* or *battle transport*.

Ammunition is calculated in issues (*Ausstattung*). A fixed ammunition scale is laid down for every unit, and it is further laid down how many rounds are to be carried with forward troops in ammunition vehicles, how many in unit light columns, and how many with divisional columns. Units make daily returns to division and division to corps. On the basis of these returns the first issue is systematically replaced as it is expended.

DIAGRAM OF SUPPLY OF AMMUNITION

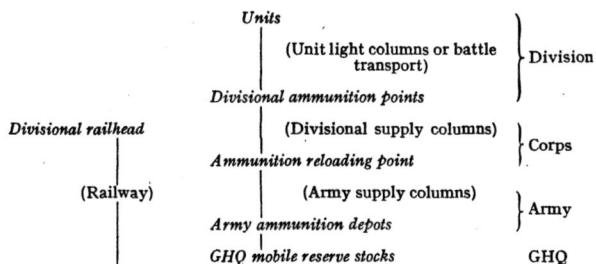

	Units	
	(Unit light columns or battle transport)	Division
	Divisional ammunition points	
Divisional railhead	(Divisional supply columns)	Corps
	Ammunition reloading point	
(Railway)	(Army supply columns)	Army
	Army ammunition depots	
	GHQ mobile reserve stocks	GHQ

4. Petrol

Responsibility is with divisional and corps technical officers (Ingenieur) and army MT officers.

(a) GHQ maintains a mobile stock of petrol on petrol trains, and petrol is forwarded from these stocks or from GHQ dumps direct to army.

(b) Army indents on GHQ. Stocks are kept either loaded on tanker trains or forward of railhead in containers in army petrol dumps (*Armee Betriebsstofflager*). Transport to these will be in army POL columns.

(c) Division indents through corps on army. One or more divisional petrol points (*Betriebsstoff-Ausgabestelle*) are appointed at which petrol is transferred from army or divisional POL columns to unit petrol lorries.

(d) In their battle transport, mechanized units include petrol lorries which receive unit fuel at divisional petrol points. Non-mechanized vehicles send their motor vehicles to be refuelled individually at divisional petrol points for single vehicles.

Petrol is calculated in *consumption units* (*Verbrauchssatz*), the consumption unit of a unit or formation being the amount required to take each of its vehicles 100 km or 60 miles. Mechanized units are, in normal circumstances, required to keep a reserve of so many consumption units.

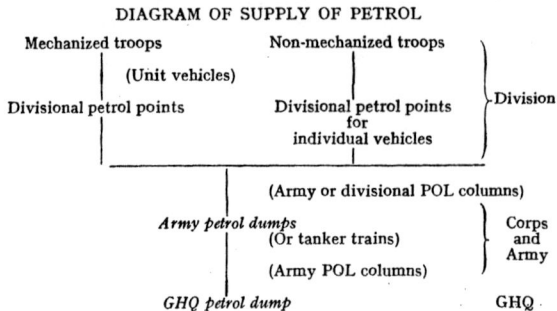

DIAGRAM OF SUPPLY OF PETROL

```
Mechanized troops              Non-mechanized troops        ⎞
                                                            |
        | (Unit vehicles)              |                    |
                                                            ├ Division
Divisional petrol points       Divisional petrol points     |
                                      for                    |
                               individual vehicles          ⎠
        |_____|_____
                              |
                              |       (Army or divisional POL columns)
                                                            ⎞
        Army petrol dumps                                   |  Corps
                    (Or tanker trains)                      ├  and
                              |                             |  Army
                              |       (Army POL columns)    ⎠
                              |
        GHQ petrol dump                        GHQ
```

Section 18.—REPAIR AND REPLACEMENT OF ARMS, EQUIPMENT, AND MT

1. Personnel

(a) *At regiment and unit.*

   (i) *Technical officers* (*Ingenieur*).—Officers at HQ (or in HQ company of mechanized regiments and units) with general charge of MT. They travel with and command the repair detachment.

   (ii) *MT officials.*—These may command repair detachments, platoons of a workshop company, etc., with title of *Werkmeister*, or may be assistants to technical officers.

   (iii) *Armourers* (*Waffenmeister*).—Officials at HQ (or in HQ company, etc.) of regiments and units, in charge of armoury for maintenance of equipment. They are assisted by an armourer NCO (*Waffenunteroffizier*).

   (iv) *NCOs IC technical equipment* with the title of *Schirrmeister*. The commonest is the MT serjeant in mechanized units. They are also found in smoke and engineer units.

(b) *At formation HQ.*

    (i) *Technical adviser for arms and equipment* (*Facharbeiter für Waffen und Gerät*).—He is a captain and is assisted by an official and two specialists (*Sachbearbeiter*). He controls the arms and equipment section and attends to the supply and maintenance of *artillery ammunition* (*see* Sec **17**, para **3**), *weapons, and equipment* (except engineer and signals equipment).

    (ii) *Technical officer* (*Divisions-* or *Korps-Ingenieur*) *for MT.*—He, together with two specialists, makes up the technical section (V), and deals exclusively with the repair and supply of MT, petrol supply, and workshops, and superintends all installations. He also collaborates with the " A " group in regard to technical personnel, and he trains MT personnel.

2. Organization of repair and maintenance units

Repair sections have, since October, 1942, been incorporated into the arm known as MT park troops (*Kraftfahrparktruppen*). From that date they wear pink as their distinguishing colour with a " J " on the shoulder straps.

(a) *Arms and equipment.*

    (i) *At units.*

        All active units include an armoury (*Waffenmeisterei*) at unit HQ or in HQ company, etc. In mechanized units the armoury forms part of the repair detachment, and in tank units of the armoured workshop company.

    (ii) *At division.*

        In an infantry division there is a workshop company which consists of 3 officers and 190 other ranks, and carries out repairs to *arms, equipment, and MT*. In an armoured division there are three mechanized workshop companies possibly grouped together as a unit performing the same duties. An armoured workshop company consists of HQ, two MT workshop platoons, and one armoury platoon.

    (iii) There are no corps workshop companies or platoons.

(iv) *At army.*

At army there are workshop companies capable of undertaking major repairs. In addition to these field workshops there are at army a number of *parks* of the various arms. They are separate units with a fixed establishment. They are largely for repair but are also holding units and may forward equipment. They include the following :—

Infantry park for all infantry weapons, including infantry guns.

Artillery park for all artillery equipment and HT vehicles.

Gas equipment park (*Gasschutzgerätepark*) for smoke as well as anti-gas equipment.

Engineer park for construction materials as well as engineer equipment.

Medical park.

Veterinary park.

(b) *MT.*

(i) *At units.*

Maintenance of individual vehicles is the duty of the driver under supervision of the company MT serjeant and unit technical officer (*see* para 1, sub-para (*a*) (i)). *Each company, etc.* (except tank squadrons, *see* (ii)) has a repair sub-section. Sub-sections may be of three kinds :—

Sub-section a. in companies, etc. with minimum of 25 vehicles (4 men).

Sub-section b. in companies, etc. with special vehicles (armoured troop carriers) (11 men).

Sub-section c. in armoured car squadrons (12 men).

At HQ of regiments and units the repair detachments are no longer standardized. Instead a detachment to fit the needs of the unit is included in the WE of unit HQ. It is commanded by the MT official or the armourer, whoever is the senior. The armoury of mechanized units is part of the repair detachment. The strength of these units is about 20 men, according to the type of unit).

(ii) *Tanks.*

A similar scheme functions for tank squadrons and battalions, viz. :—

Section a. to squadrons (17 men).
Section b. to battalions (7 men).

At tank regiment HQ there is an armoured workshop company (*Panzerwerkstattkompanie*) consisting of three workshop platoons, a recovery platoon, armoury, signals workshop, and transport.

(iii) *At division.*

Workshop company which carries out repairs to arms, equipment, and MT (*see* para 2 (*a*) (ii)).

(iv) *At army.*

In addition to the army workshop companies there is an army MT park (para 2 (*a*) (iv)). To supplement this park certain specialist units can be allotted by GHQ to army. They are :—

Central spare parts depot (*Zentral-Ersatzteillager*).
Tyre depot (*Reifenlager*).
Tank spare parts depots (*Panzer-Ersatzteillager*).

Track depots (*Gleiskettenlager*), etc., etc.

To facilitate the transport of these spare parts, the following separate units may be allotted :—

Tank spare parts columns (*Panzer-Ersatzteilkolonne*).
Spare parts echelons (*Nachschubstaffel für Ersatzteile*).

3. Replacement of arms, equipment, and MT

(*a*) *Arms and equipment.*

(i) Army indents through GHQ on the head of army supply for weapons and anti-gas equipment. Equipment, when brought from the home area, is taken by army columns either to an *army park* or an *equipment collecting point* (*Armee-Gerätesammelstelle*) which is set up by the technical adviser and manned by personnel of the army supply battalions. Each is, as the name suggests, primarily for salvage, but is also one of the channels through which equipment is forwarded.

(ii) Division indents through corps on army. In the same way, a *divisional equipment collecting point*, manned by the supply company, is set up. Equipment is brought up on army, corps, or divisional columns, or in divisional columns from divisional railhead.

(iii) Units indent on division and collect equipment in their vehicles from divisional equipment collecting points.

DIAGRAM SHOWING SUPPLY OF ARMS AND EQUIPMENT

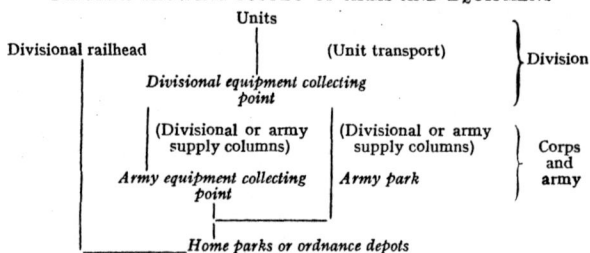

Units

Divisional railhead   (Unit transport)   Division

Divisional equipment collecting point

(Divisional or army supply columns)   (Divisional or army supply columns)   Corps and army

Army equipment collecting point   *Army park*

Home parks or ordnance depots

(b) *MT*.

(i) GHQ receives and forwards indents from army. Vehicles will be received by army from GHQ at the army MT park. Supply may be direct from the home area, but it is probably in general through GHQ parks.

(ii) Division indents through corps on army. There is no special organization for delivering MT and spare parts to units. They go either through the equipment collecting centres or by the same channels as petrol (*see* Sec 17, para 4).

Section 19.—MEDICAL SERVICES

1. **Personnel.**

(a) *At unit.*

At battalion HQ there is a battalion MO with an assistant or auxiliary MO (*Assistenzarzt* or *Hilfs-arzt*). In addition there is a medical NCO and a stretcher-bearer at each rifle company HQ and a stretcher-bearer at each platoon HQ. In parachute battalions it is believed that there is an MO with each company, while each platoon has a trained medical orderly. The MO with a tank battalion travels in a specially adapted armoured car with the AFVs of the battalion.

(b) **At formation HQ.**

At regimental HQ there is a senior MO (*Divisions-arzt*). He is responsible for supervising the employment of the battalion medical services and the evacuation of sick and wounded. At higher formation HQ there is a director of medical services whose section is numbered IVb and who works closely with the second GSO (Ib). He is assisted by a MO (*Stabsarzt*), two medical other ranks, and two clerks.

2. Organization of medical services

(a) *At division.*

The medical units within a division are as follows :—

Divisional field hospital (not in armoured divisions).
Medical company or companies.
MT ambulance platoons.

Details are as follows :—

(i) *The divisional field hospital.*

This is primarily intended for reception and retention of casualties requiring urgent operations, or whose condition will not permit of further evacuation without a period of rest and resuscitation. It is completely mechanized and fully equipped. Its capacity is 200 casualties and it can be set up in three hours.

(ii) *The medical company.*

There are usually two medical companies in a division. Usually one is mechanized, and in many divisions both are mechanized. On the march or short halts it establishes one or more casualty clearing posts. In billets where the stay is likely to be more than three to four nights, it sets up temporary hospitals as far as possible in conjunction with local civilian hospitals.

In action the three platoons of the company have definite responsibilities. One platoon is responsible for establishing a field dressing station (FDS) and a lightly wounded collecting post (LWCP), the second is the stretcher bearer (SB) platoon, the third is held in reserve. An ambulance car post may also be formed depending on whether ambulances go forward to battalion aid posts or not.

(iii) *The MT ambulance platoons.*

Two of these are attached to field hospitals in infantry and mountain divisions. In motorized and armoured divisions there are three. They are employed in evacuating casualties from the FDS to the field hospital, or from either of these and the LWCP to the Casualty Collecting Post (CCP) established by army ambulance units (*see* sub-para (*c*)). These each comprise approximately 18 vehicles and 42 all ranks.

(*b*) *At corps.*

No medical units are allotted. It is customary, however, for DMS Army to place various medical units at the disposal of the DMS Corps before an action.

(*c*) *At army.*

The army medical unit comprises :—

Medical companies.
Field hospital detachments.
MT ambulance sections.

The medical companies reinforce or relieve those of divisions as required. The field hospital detachments carry out functions similar to those of the divisional field hospitals. The MT ambulance sections are normally employed in evacuating sick and wounded through CCPs which they set up at railheads, ports, and other traffic centres in which wounded and sick are accommodated, while waiting evacuation to hospitals in rear.

3. System of evacuation of casualties (*see* diagram).

(*a*) Speed is of paramount importance. To ensure that it shall be achieved, the stretcher-bearer platoon of the medical company assists the battalion stretcher-bearers in collection of wounded, and sometimes specially trained dogs are used to help find casualties.

(*b*) (i) The casualty receives first-aid treatment in the battalion post. If able to walk he goes to the LWCP (*see* (v)).

(ii) Stretcher cases are evacuated by ambulances which come to the battalion aid post, or by stretcher-bearers to ambulance car post.

(iii) From ambulance car post the ambulance casualty goes to the field dressing station, where emergency operations are carried out.

(iv) If further treatment is necessary, he is then evacuated to the divisional field hospital and thence to army field hospitals, probably via the casualty collecting post.

(v) A casualty able to make his way to the LWCP is evacuated to the CCP unless his condition deteriorates, when he is passed to the field dressing station and normal evacuation. From the CCP he is evacuated to an army field hospital for lightly wounded.

(vi) The casualty, who may have recovered sufficiently at FDS, may not warrant evacuation to the divisional field hospital. If so, the casualty will go direct to the CCP and thence to the army field hospital for lightly wounded.

(vii) Evacuation from army field hospitals is to hospitals in GERMANY and occupied countries.

DIAGRAM SHOWING STAGES OF EVACUATION

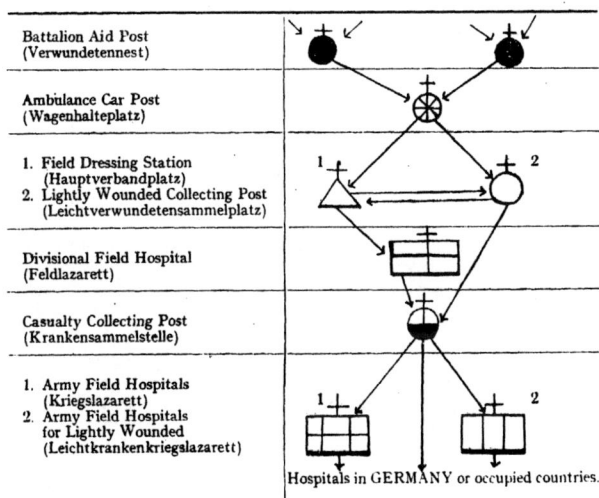

Battalion Aid Post (Verwundetennest)	
Ambulance Car Post (Wagenhalteplatz)	
1. Field Dressing Station (Hauptverbandplatz) 2. Lightly Wounded Collecting Post (Leichtverwundetensammelplatz)	
Divisional Field Hospital (Feldlazarett)	
Casualty Collecting Post (Krankensammelstelle)	
1. Army Field Hospitals (Kriegslazarett) 2. Army Field Hospitals for Lightly Wounded (Leichtkrankenkriegslazarett)	

Hospitals in GERMANY or occupied countries.

SECTION 20.—**THE VETERINARY SERVICES**

1. Personnel.

(a) *At regimental HQ* there is a veterinary officer, but seldom at a unit.

(b) *At regiments* there is a farrier, or farrier NCO, but seldom more than one at a unit.

(c) *At divisional HQ* there are two officers who are responsible for veterinary administration, the divisional veterinary officer assisted by the HQ veterinary officer (*Stabs-Veterinär*). At army there is a similar section, but the exact number of officers at army is not known.

2. Organization of veterinary services.

(a) *At division*

There is the divisional veterinary company which consists of :—

    (i) Collecting section (*Sammelstaffel*).

    (ii) Hospital section (*Lazarettstaffel*).

    (iii) Stores section (*Vorratsstaffel*).

(b) *At army.* (There are no corps veterinary units.)

There are army veterinary hospitals (*Pferde-lazarett*), veterinary depots, and army HT columns.

3. System of evacuation and supply of horses.

(a) At division the veterinary company has the following duties :—

    (i) To treat horses which are wounded or fall sick in the divisional area.

    (ii) To provide units with remounts.

    (iii) To supply units with veterinary stores and shoeing implements.

It may be called upon to establish in the forward areas one or more veterinary depots, which serve as delivery points for remounts and veterinary stores.

(b) At army veterinary hospitals, sick horses received from the divisional veterinary companies are treated, and purchased, requisitioned, or captured horses are received. Horses which have been cured and are fit for service are delivered to veterinary depots (*Pferdepark*). Horses which need lengthy treatment are evacuated to veterinary hospitals at home. If the distance between the divisional veterinary companies and army veterinary hospitals is too great, veterinary evacuating stations (*Pferde-sammelplätz*) are set up in the forward areas under army arrangements. These stations are equipped with the necessary personnel and stores for treating sick and wounded horses.

The army horsed transport columns evacuate sick horses from the divisional veterinary companies to army veterinary hospitals (*via* the veterinary evacuating stations if established). They also deliver remounts from army veterinary depots to the divisional veterinary companies.

Diagram of Evacuation and Supply of Horses

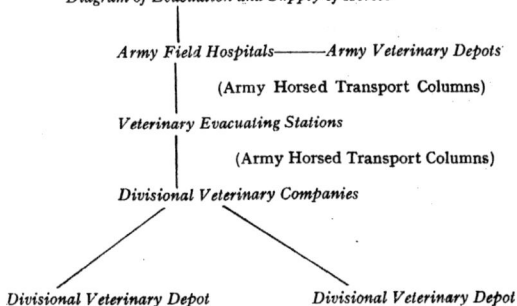

Army Field Hospitals————*Army Veterinary Depots*

(Army Horsed Transport Columns)

Veterinary Evacuating Stations

(Army Horsed Transport Columns)

Divisional Veterinary Companies

Divisional Veterinary Depot   *Divisional Veterinary Depot*

SECTION 21.—THE PROVOST SERVICES (ORDNUNGSDIENST)

1. The military police (Feldgendarmerie).

Units of military police are employed with divisions and higher formations. They wear orange piping and have on the left upper arm the Nazi eagle and swastika surrounded by an oak wreath, on the left lower arm a brown band inscribed with the word "*Feldgendarmerie*" in silver. When on duty MPs wear a metal plate (*Ringkragen*) on a chain round their necks. They perform similar functions to our own MPs. They are organized into battalions of three companies, each of three platoons. A typical company consists of 4 officers, 90 NCOs, and 22 men, with 22 lorries, 7 trucks, and 28 MCs.

Establishments provide various types of MP detachments which are self-contained units under command of divisions. They work in close co-operation with the secret field police (*Geheime Feldpolizei*) and with district commanders and town majors.

2. Secret field police (Geheime Feldpolizei GFP).

The officers of the GFP wear the uniform of the army official with light blue piping and on the shoulder strap the letters GFP in brass or yellow metal. The NCOs and men may wear either GAF or infantry uniform also with the letters GFP on the shoulder straps. They are mostly recruited from the GESTAPO and are permitted to wear mufti and on occasions any uniform they may wish to wear in pursuance of their duties, and in addition they have power of command over all NCOs and other ranks.

Their duties have been laid down as :—

(a) The pursuit and arrest of traitors, spies, saboteurs ; the combating of enemy propaganda.

(b) The general execution of all security protection measures.

(c) To act as security advisers, principally to the intelligence officer.

PART II

ORGANIZATION OF DIVISIONS

PREFACE

1. There is no war establishment for any type of German division. Each division is formed in accordance with a secret order from the War Ministry (*Oberkommando des Heeres*—rear echelon) which specifies the war establishments that are to be used for the various sub-units. Important variations must therefore be expected from division to division.

2. In a work of the scope of the present Pocket Book, it is not possible to do more than set out the war establishment of typical divisions.

3. It is the duty of intelligence staffs in the field to make every effort to ascertain as soon as possible how far the actual war establishment of a formation, with which they are in contact, differs from the typical war establishment given in this book.

4. It is also a common German practice to re-group the forces available in a given theatre of war. These re-groupings may be purely temporary, designed to meet the tactical requirements of a particular operation, or they may acquire a quasi-permanent character when they are dictated by heavy losses in personnel and equipment (as in Libya), or by the peculiarity of terrain and the lack of more suitable forces (as in Tunisia).

5. For these reasons, intelligence staffs in Libya and Tunisia found it necessary to build up the Order of Battle and organization of the German forces by collating detailed information about the component sub-units of these forces.

6. Intelligence officers in the field may therefore find it useful to keep a separate loose leaf note-book arranged on the same lines as this Pocket Book, with the known details of the organization of the units with which they are in contact. Alternatively these details might be inserted at the appropriate places in this Pocket Book on sheets of paper cut to the correct size.

Note.—Where in the tables that follow the abbreviation " WT " is used, it is to be taken as meaning wireless generally, except where the abbreviation " RT " is used in addition.

CHAPTER 1

SECTION 22.—INFANTRY DIVISION

The infantry division consists of :—

The table facing page **46** shows the organization of the infantry division in outline, and a summary of personnel, weapons, and vehicles in the infantry division is given in the table on the reverse.

TABLE 1

SIGNALS BATTALION IN AN INFANTRY DIVISION

Bn HQ (part mech)

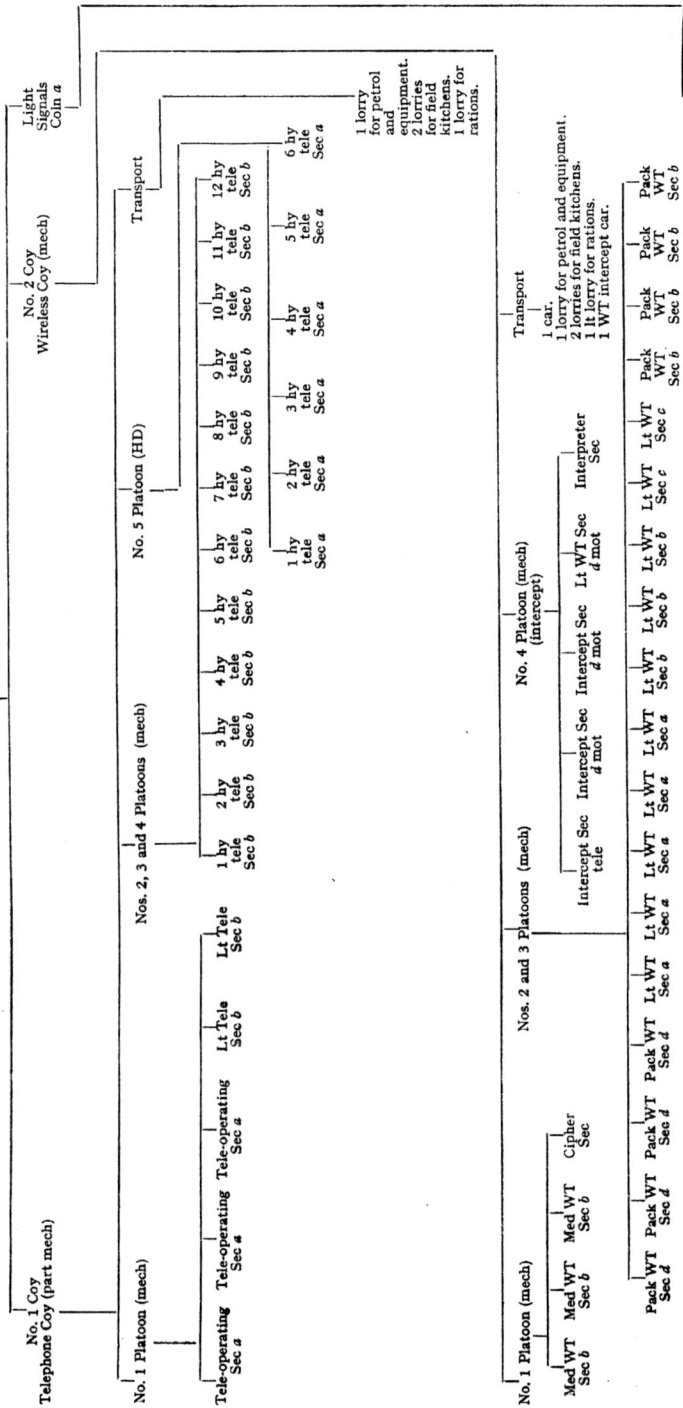

No. 1 Coy
Telephone Coy (part mech)

No. 2 Coy
Wireless Coy (mech)

Light
Signals
Coln a

No. 1 Coy Telephone Coy (part mech)

No. 1 Platoon (mech)

Tele-operating Sec a
Tele-operating Sec a
Tele-operating Sec a
Lt Tele Sec b
Lt Tele Sec b

Nos. 2, 3 and 4 Platoons (mech)

1 hy tele Sec b
2 hy tele Sec b
3 hy tele Sec b
4 hy tele Sec b
5 hy tele Sec b
6 hy tele Sec b

Transport

No. 5 Platoon (HD)

6 hy tele Sec b
7 hy tele Sec b
8 hy tele Sec b
9 hy tele Sec b
10 hy tele Sec b
11 hy tele Sec b
12 hy tele Sec b

1 hy tele Sec a
1 hy tele Sec a
2 hy tele Sec a
3 hy tele Sec a
4 hy tele Sec a
5 hy tele Sec a
6 hy tele Sec a

1 lorry for petrol and equipment.
2 lorries for field kitchens.
1 lorry for rations.

No. 2 Coy Wireless Coy (mech)

No. 1 Platoon (mech)

Med WT Sec b
Med WT Sec b
Med WT Sec b
Cipher Sec

Pack WT Sec d
Pack WT Sec d
Pack WT Sec d
Pack WT Sec d

Nos. 2 and 3 Platoons (mech)

Intercept Sec tele
Lt WT Sec a
Lt WT Sec a
Lt WT Sec a
Lt WT Sec b
Lt WT Sec b

Intercept Sec d mot
Intercept Sec d mot
Interpreter Sec

No. 4 Platoon (mech)
(intercept)

Lt WT Sec b
Lt WT Sec b
Lt WT Sec c
Lt WT Sec c
Lt WT d mot
Lt WT d mot

Transport

1 car.
1 lorry for petrol and equipment.
2 lorries for field kitchens.
1 lt lorry for rations.
1 WT intercept car.

Pack WT Sec b
Pack WT Sec b
Pack WT Sec b
Pack WT Sec b

Light Signals Coln a

1 Signals repair lorry.
1 Signals repair equipment lorry.
1 car.
1 petrol lorry.
1 equipment lorry.
3 tele-equipment lorries.
1 WT equipment lorry.
1 LMG.

STRENGTH

	Personnel	MT	MC	HD vehicles	Horses	LMGs
Bn HQ ...	24	5	2	—	4	—
Telephone Coy ...	243	45	15	7	48	10
Wireless Coy ...	171	44	13	—	—	6
Light Signals Coln a ...	36	9	2	—	—	1
Total ...	474	103	32	7	52	17

RECONNAISSANCE UNIT IN AN INFANTRY DIVISION

TABLE 2

HQ

Signal Pl

3 pack W/T sets Horsed (Type b) | 1 pack W/T set Mech (Type b) | 1 small W/T set | 1 med W/T set | 1 pack receiving set

Sabre Sqn

HQ — Sabre Tp | Sabre Tp | Sabre Tp (Each 3 LMGs) — MG Tp 2 MMGs

HQ — MMG Tp 4 MMGs

Recce Sqn

HQ — LMG Tp | LMG Tp | LMG Tp | LMG Tp (Each 3 LMGs One 5-cm (2-in) mortar) — MMG Tp 2 MMGs

Inf Gun Tp 2 inf guns | A tk Tp 3 A tk guns, 2 LMGs | Armd Car Tp 3 lt armd cars

Heavy Sqn

Med Mortar Tp Three 8-cm (3-in) mortars

Strength : 575 all ranks.

Fire-power :

LMGs	... ...	23
MMGs	... ...	8
2-cm (·79-in) AA/A tk guns	...	3
5-cm (1·97-in) A tk guns	...	3
5-cm (2-in) mortars	...	3
8-cm (3-in) mortars	...	3
7·5-cm (2·95-in) inf guns	...	2
Armd Cars	... ...	3

NOTE.—In place of a recce unit, organized as above, infantry divisions may have :—

(a) a recce unit (formerly known as " cyclist unit ") as in the mtn div (*see* page 69), or consisting of two recce (*i.e.* cyclist) coys, or

(b) a mobile unit (schnelle Abteilung), consisting of two recce (*i.e.* cyclist) coys, or one recce coy and one sabre sqn ; and two A tk companies (of which one or both may be equipped with SP guns).

TABLE 3

INFANTRY REGIMENT IN AN INFANTRY DIVISION

(a) *Organization*

H.Q.

HQ Coy — Sig Pl | Mtd Inf Pl | MCDR Pl | Pnr Pl

I Bn | II Bn | III Bn

13 Inf Gun Coy — Six 7·5-cm (2·95-in) inf guns, Two 15-cm (5·91-in) inf guns

14 A tk Coy — Each three 5-cm (1·97-in) A tk guns 2 LMGs

Lt Inf Col

HQ | Sig Pl | 1 Rifle Coy | 2 Rifle Coy | 3 Rifle Coy | 4 MG Coy

HQ | Pl | Pl | Pl

1 Rifle Coy — Each 1 LMG

3 Rifle Coy — A tk rifle sec — 3 A tk rifles; Lt Mortar Sec — One 5-cm (2-in) mortar

HQ | Sec | Sec | Sec | Sec | Sec

4 MG Coy — HQ | MG Pl | MG Pl | MG Pl | Med Mortar Pl

MG Pl — HQ | MMG Sec | MMG Sec — Each 2 MMGs

Med Mortar Pl — HQ | Sec | Sec | Sec

Sec — Sub-Sec | Sub-Sec — Each one 8-cm (3-in mortar)

NOTES.— (1) In some reg HQ coys the mtd inf pls replaced by a cyclist pl.

(ii) The 14th A tk coy may have one or more pls equipped with 7·5-cm (2·95-in) A tk guns.

INFANTRY REGIMENT IN AN INFANTRY DIVISION

(b) *Strength and fire-power*

	Strength (approx)	LMGs	MMGs	A tk rifles	5-cm (2-in) mortars	8-cm (3-in) mortars	5-cm (1·97-in) A tk guns	7·5-cm (2·95-in) inf guns	15-cm (5·91-in) inf guns
Regt	3,215	118	36	27	27	18	9	6	2
Bn	854	36	12	9	9	6	—	—	—
Rifle Coy	191	12	—	3	3	—	—	—	—
MG Coy	202	—	12	—	—	6	—	—	—
13 Inf Gun Coy	200	—	—	—	—	—	—	6	2
14 A tk Coy	153	6	—	—	—	—	9	—	—

ARTILLERY REGIMENT IN AN INFANTRY DIVISION

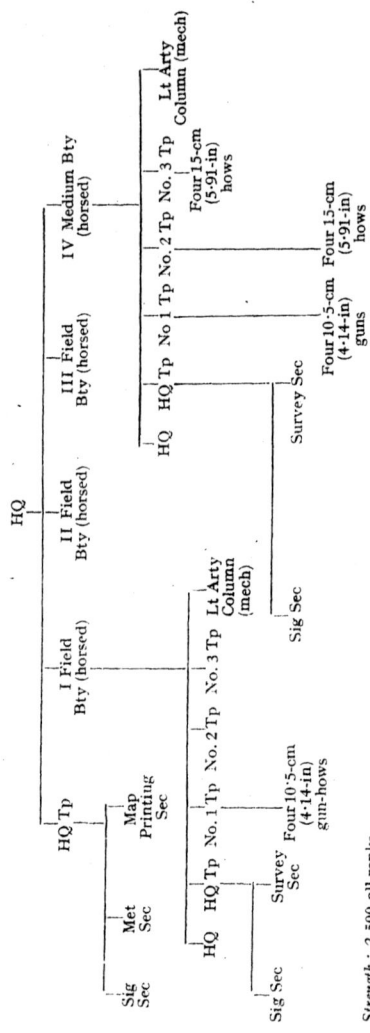

TABLE 4

HQ

Sig Sec — Met Sec — Map Printing Sec — HQ Tp

I Field Bty (horsed) — II Field Bty (horsed) — III Field Bty (horsed) — IV Medium Bty (horsed)

Sig Sec — HQ — Survey Sec — No 1 Tp — No 2 Tp — No 3 Tp — Lt Arty Column (mech)

Four 10·5-cm (4·14-in) gun-hows

Sig Sec — HQ — Survey Sec — No 1 Tp — No 2 Tp — No 3 Tp — Lt Arty Column (mech)

Four 10·5-cm (4·14-in) guns

Four 15-cm (5·91-in) hows

Four 15-cm (5·91-in) hows

Strength : 2,500 all ranks.
Fire-power : LMGs 24
10·5-cm (4·14-in) gun-hows ... 36
10·5-cm (4·14-in) guns 4
15-cm (5·91-in) hows 8

NOTES.— (i) Each Tp has 2 LMGs.
(ii) The Med Bty may be equipped throughout with 15-cm (5·91-in) hows.
(iii) The Arty Regts of some 20 Inf Divs formed since December, 1941, include a Tp of six or eight 15-cm (5·91-in) smoke mortars 41.

TABLE 5

ANTI-TANK BATTALION IN AN INFANTRY DIVISION

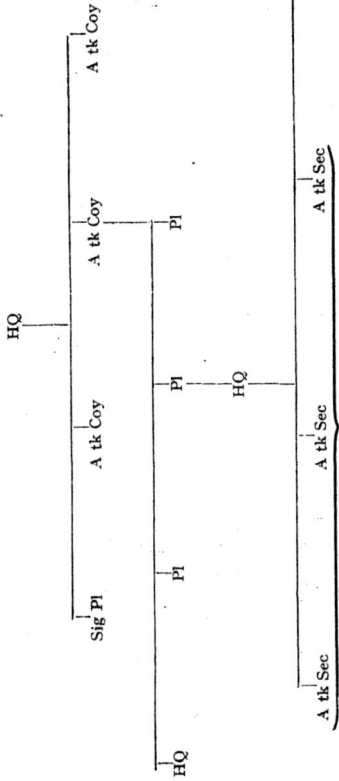

HQ

Sig Pl   A tk Coy   A tk Coy   A tk Coy

HQ   Pl

HQ   Pl   Pl

A tk Sec   A tk Sec   A tk Sec

LMG Sec
2 LMGs

Each one 5-cm (1·97-in) or 7·5-cm (2·95-in) A tk gun

Strength: 550 all ranks.

Fire-power: 5-cm (1·97-in) or 7·5-cm (2·95-in) A tk guns 27

LMGs 18

NOTES.— (i) The third A tk Coy is in some cases replaced by an AA Coy with three platoons, each of four 2-cm (·79-in) AA/A tk guns SP and 1 LMG.

(ii) Battalions may have one or more SP companies, equipped with 7·5-cm (2·95-in) or 7·62-cm (2·99-in) A tk guns on Pz Kw II or Pz Kw 38 (t) chassis.

TABLE 6

ENGINEER BATTALION IN AN INFANTRY DIVISION

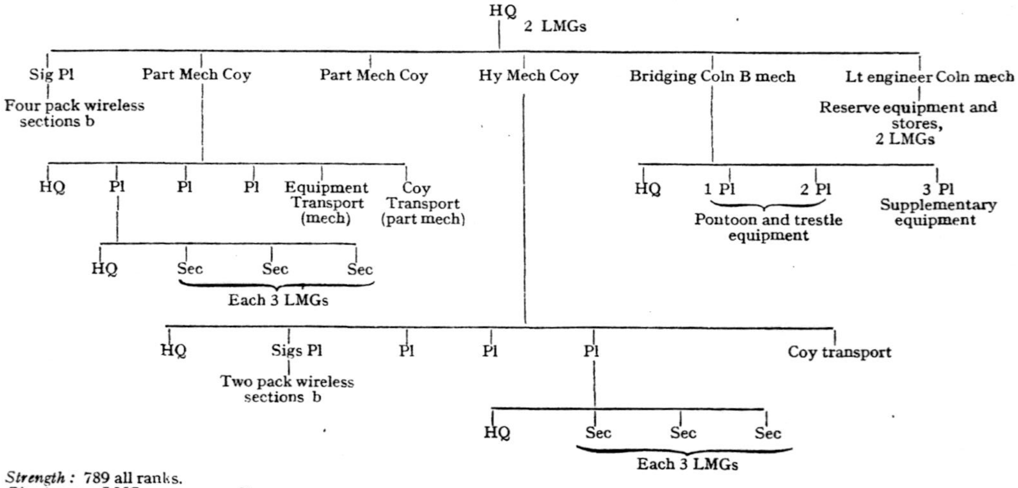

HQ 2 LMGs

Sig Pl
Four pack wireless sections b

Part Mech Coy

Part Mech Coy

Hy Mech Coy

Bridging Coln B mech

Lt engineer Coln mech
Reserve equipment and stores, 2 LMGs

HQ

Pl

Pl

Pl

Equipment Transport (mech)

Coy Transport (part mech)

Sec Sec Sec
Each 3 LMGs

HQ

Sigs Pl
Two pack wireless sections b

Pl

Pl

Pl

Coy transport

HQ

Pl

Sec Sec Sec
Each 3 LMGs

HQ

1 Pl

2 Pl
Pontoon and trestle equipment

3 Pl
Supplementary equipment

Strength: 789 all ranks.
Fire-power: LMGs... ... 31

NOTE.—In place of bridging column B, some battalions probably still have a bridging column C.

TABLE 7

SERVICES OF AN INFANTRY DIVISION

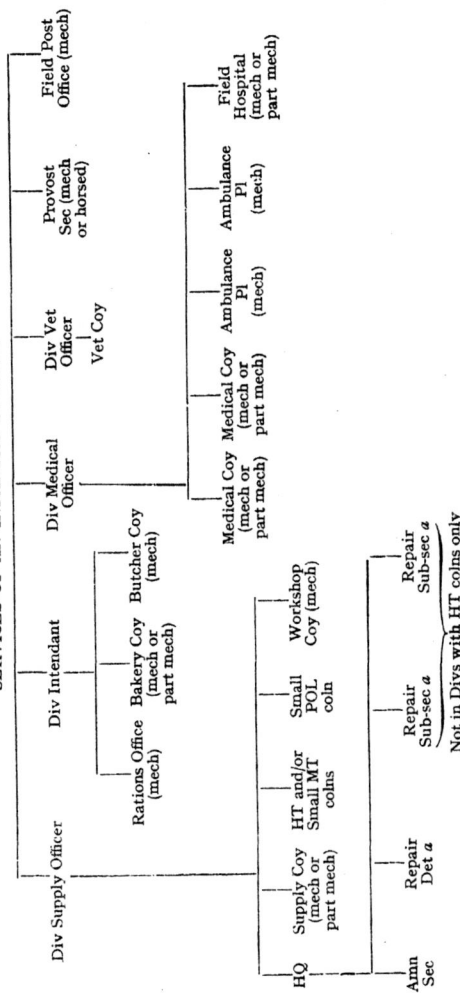

Div Supply Officer

- Div Intendant
  - Rations Office (mech)
  - Bakery Coy (mech or part mech)
  - Butcher Coy (mech)
- Div Medical Officer
  - Medical Coy (mech or part mech)
  - Medical Coy (mech or part mech)
    - Ambulance Pl (mech)
    - Ambulance Pl (mech)
      - Field Hospital (mech or part mech)
- Div Vet Officer
  - Vet Coy
- Provost Sec (mech or horsed)
- Field Post Office (mech)

HQ

- Supply Coy (mech or part mech)
  - Repair Det *a*
- HT and/or Small MT colns
  - Repair Sub-sec *a*
- Small POL coln
- Workshop Coy (mech)
  - Repair Sub-sec *a*

Amn Sec

Not in Divs with HT colns only

Strength: 2,205 all ranks (average mechanization).
Fire-power: 30 LMGs.

NOTE.—The armament of the services for local defence varies considerably. 30 LMGs is a typical allotment for services organized as above. A certain number of 2-cm (·79-in) AA/A tk guns may also be included.

TABLE 8

INFANTRY DIVISION

Divisional HQ

Main branches: Recce Unit | Sigs Bn | Inf Regt | Inf Regt | Arty Regt | A tk Bn | Eng Bn | Divisional Services

Recce Unit

Sigs Pl

- **Sabre Sqn** — 9 LMGs, 2 MMGs
- **Cyclist Sqn** — 9 LMGs, 2 MMGs, 3 Lt mortars
- **Hy Sqn** — 7 LMGs, 4 MMGs, 2×7·5-cm (2·95-in) inf guns, 3×5-cm (1·97-in) A tk guns, 3×8-cm (3-in) mortars, 3 lt armd cars

Sigs Bn

- HQ (part mech)
- No. 1 Tele Coy (part mech) 10 LMGs
- No. 2 W/T Coy (mech) 6 LMGs
- Light Signals Coln 1 LMG

Inf Regt

Regt HQ

- HQ Coy
  - MCDR Pl
  - Sigs Pl
  - Pnr Pl 3 LMGs
- I Bn
- II Bn
- III Bn
  - HQ
  - 9 Rifle Coy
  - 10 Rifle Coy
  - 11 Rifle Coy — Each 12 LMGs, 3 A tk rifles, 3×5-cm (2-in) mortars
  - 12 MG Coy — 12 MMGs, 6×8-cm (3-in) mortars
  - 13 Inf gun Coy — 6×7·5-cm (2·95-in) inf guns, 2×15-cm (5·91-in) inf guns
- 14 A tk Coy — 9×5-cm (1·97-in) A tk guns, 6 LMGs
- Lt Inf Coln 1 LMG

Inf Regt

Regt HQ

Arty Regt

Regt HQ

- HQ Tp
- No. 1 Fd Bty
- No. 2 Fd Bty
- No. 3 Fd Bty
  - Bty HQ
  - HQ Tp
  - Tp Tp Tp Tp — Each 4×10·5-cm (4·14-in) gun hows, 2 LMGs
  - Survey Sec
  - Sigs Pl
- No. 4 Med Bty
  - Bty HQ
  - HQ Tp
  - Tp Tp Tp — Each 4×15-cm (5·91-in) hows, 2 LMGs
  - Survey Sec
  - Sigs Pl
- Lt Arty Coln (mech)
- Lt Arty Coln (mech)
  - Tp — 4×10·5-cm (4·14-in) guns, 2 LMGs

A tk Bn

- HQ
- Sigs Pl
- A tk Coy
  - Pl
  - Pl
  - Pl
- A tk Coy
  - Pl
  - Pl
  - Pl — Each three 5-cm (1·97-in) A tk guns, 2 LMGs
- A tk or AA Coy with 12×2-cm (·79-in) AA/A tk guns, 4 LMGs

Eng Bn

HQ 2 LMGs

- Br Coln B (mech)
  - HQ
  - Coy (part mech)
  - Coy (part mech) — Each 9 LMGs
  - Hy Mech Coy 9 LMGs
  - Sigs Pl
  - 1 Pl
  - 2 Pl — Pontoon and Trestle Equipment
  - 3 Pl — Supplementary Equipment

Divisional Services

- Lt Eng Coln — Reserve Equipment and Stores 2 LMGs

[to face page 46]

INFANTRY DIVISION—SUMMARY OF PERSONNEL, WEAPONS AND VEHICLES

Unit	Personnel	Armd cars	Small arms			AA and/or A tk guns		Mortars		Close Support Artillery		Divisional Artillery			MV	MC	HT	Horses
			LMGs	MMGs	A tk rifles	2-cm (·79-in) AA/ A tk guns	5-cm (1·97-in) A tk guns	5-cm (2-in) mortars	8-cm (3-in) mortars	7·5-cm (2·95-in) inf guns	15-cm (5·91-in) inf guns	10·5-cm (4·14-in) gun hows	10·5-cm (4·14-in) guns	15-cm (5·91-in) bows				
Div HQ … …	152	—	—	2	—	—	—	—	—	—	—	—	—	—	30	17	—	20
Div Sig Bn …	474	—	17	—	—	—	—	—	—	—	—	—	—	—	103	32	7	32
Recce unit …	575	3	23	8	—	3	3	3	3	2	—	—	—	—	33	45	3	213
Div Infantry …	9,645	—	354	108	81	—	27	81	54	18	6	—	—	—	245	140	650	2,109
Arty Regt …	2,500	—	24	—	—	—	—	—	—	—	—	36	4	8	135	40	238	1,789
A tk Bn… …	550	—	18 (16)	—	—	— (12)	27 (18)	—	—	—	—	—	—	—	95	45	—	—
Eng Bn …	789	—	31	—	—	—	—	—	—	—	—	—	—	—	85	44	19	52
Services (average mech)	2,205	—	30	—	—	—	—	—	—	—	—	—	—	—	234	88	234	705
TOTAL (average mech)	16,890	3	497 (495)	118	81	3 (15)	57 (48)	84	57	20	6	36	4	8	960	451	1,151	4,940

	Personnel	MV	MC	HT	Horses
TOTAL (minimum mechanization) … …	17,359	873	436	1,420	5,621
TOTAL (average mechanization) …	16,890	960	451	1,151	4,940
TOTAL (maximum mechanization) … …	16,563	1,052	464	934	4,423

NOTE.—(i) *A tk bn.*—Figures in brackets are for a battalion of which the third Coy is an AA Coy.

CHAPTER 2

Section 23.—MOTORIZED DIVISION

The motorized division consists of :—

The table facing page 56 shows the organization of the motorized division in outline and a summary of personnel, AFVs, weapons, and MT in the motorized division is given in the table on the reverse.

SIGNALS BATTALION IN A MOTORIZED DIVISION   TABLE 9

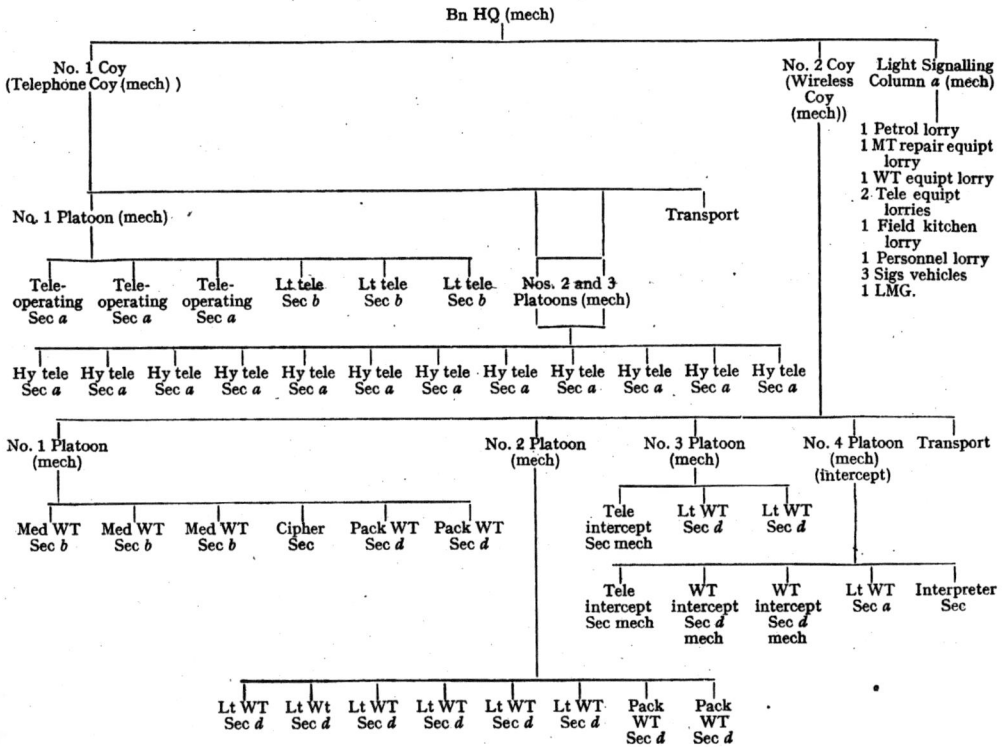

STRENGTH

	Personnel	MC	MT	LMGs
Bn HQ	40	3	10	—
Telephone Coy ...	220	14	42	8
Wireless Coy ...	160	15	46	8
Light Sig Coln *a* ...	36	1	9	1
TOTAL ...	456	33	107	17

TABLE 10

ARMOURED RECONNAISSANCE UNIT IN A MOTORIZED DIVISION

HQ (2 LMGs)

Branches under HQ: **Sig Pl — Armd C Sqn — Armd Recce Coy — Armd Recce Coy — Armd Recce Coy — Hy Coy — Lt Coln (3 LMGs)**

Sig Pl:
- Lt telephone sec C (mech)
- 2 pack WT secs (mech)
- Lt armd WT sec C (mech)
- 3 med armd WT secs b (mech)
- 4 lt armd WT secs d (mech)

Armd Recce Coy:
- A tk Pl
- Three 5-cm (1·97-in) A tk guns
- Three 2·8-cm (1·1-in) A tk guns
- 2 LMGs

Hy Coy:
- HQ
- Lt Inf Gun Pl — Two 7·5-cm (2·95-in) inf guns
- Pnr Pl — 3 LMGs

Armd C Sqn:
- HQ
- Hy Tp — Sec, Sec — Each 2 hy armd cars
- Lt Tp, Lt Tp, Lt Tp, Lt Tp — Sec, Sec, Sec — Each 3 lt armd cars

Armd Recce Coy (lower):
- HQ
- Pl, Pl, Pl — Sec, Sec, Sec — Each 2 lt armd cars
- Hy Pl
- HQ — MMG Sec, MMG Sec — Each 2 MMGs
- Med Mortar Sec — Two 8-cm (3-in) mortars

1 A tk rifle

Strength: 1,140 all ranks.

Fire-power:

LMGs ...	88
MMGs ...	12
A tk rifles ...	9
2·8-cm (1·1-in) A tk guns ...	3
5-cm (1·97-in) A tk guns ...	3
8-cm (3-in) mortars ...	6
7·5 cm (2·95-in) inf guns ...	2
2-cm (·79-in) guns ...	18
or	
2-cm (·79-in) guns ...	12 and
7·5-cm (2·95-in) tk guns ...	6

NOTES.—(i) *Armd C Sqn*: The allotment of the various types of armoured cars is not fixed. The following is the allotment upon which the fire-power shown is based:—

6 hy armd cars each with one 2-cm (·79-in) A tk or 7·5-cm (2·95-in) tk gun and 1 LMG.
6 lt armd cars with WT and 1 LMG.
12 lt armd cars with one 2-cm (·79-in) AA/A tk gun and 1 LMG.

(ii) *Fire-power*: The fire-power shown for the unit is based on the assumption that all three armd recce coys are transported in "Volkswagen" or on MC. For each armd recce coy transported in armd carriers, the fire-power shown will probably be increased by three 3·7-cm (1·45-in) A tk guns and 16 LMGs.

TABLE 11

MOTORIZED INFANTRY REGIMENT IN A MOTORIZED DIVISION

HQ

HQ Coy — Sig Pl — MCDR Pl
  MC Pl (3 LMGs)
  Pnr Pl (3 LMGs)

I Bn — II Bn — III Bn — 13 Inf Gun Coy — 14 A tk Coy — Lt Inf Coln

13 Inf Gun Coy:
HQ — Pl — Pl — Pl
Six 7·5-cm (2·95-in) inf guns
Two 15-cm (5·91-in) inf guns

14 A tk Coy:
Each three 5-cm (1·97-in) A tk guns 2 LMGs

I Bn:
HQ — Sig Pl — 1 Rifle Coy — 2 Rifle Coy — 3 Rifle Coy — 4 MG Coy

1 Rifle Coy:
HQ — Pl — Pl — Pl — A tk rifle Sec 3 A tk rifles — Lt Mortar Sec One 5-cm mortar (2-in)

Pl:
Sec — Sec — Sec
Each 1 LMG

4 MG Coy:
HQ — MG Pl — MG Pl — MG Pl — Med Mortar Pl

MG Pl:
HQ — MMG Sec — MMG Sec
Each 2 MMGs.

Med Mortar Pl:
HQ — Sec — Sec
  Sub-sec — Sub-sec
  Each one 8-cm (3-in) mortar

Strength (approx) 3,100 all ranks.
Fire-power:

LMGs	120
MMGs	36
A tk rifles	27
5-cm (1·97-in) A tk guns ...	9
5-cm (2-in) mortars ...	27
8-cm (3-in) mortars ...	18
7·5-cm (2·95-in) inf guns ...	6
15-cm (5·91-in) inf guns ...	2

NOTE.—The 14th A tk coy may have one or more pls equipped with 7·5-cm (2·95-in) A tk guns.

TANK BATTALION IN A MOTORIZED DIVISION

TABLE 12

HQ

HQ Sqn	Lt Sqn	Lt Sqn	Lt Sqn	Med Sqn	Workshop Coy

HQ Sqn — Sig Pl 1 Pz Kw III, 2 Hy ACV

Lt Sqn:
- Lt Tk Tp 7 Pz Kw II
- Pnr Pl 3 LMGs
- MC Pl 4 LMGs
- AA Pl 8 MGs

HQ 2 Pz Kw III

Each 5 Pz Kw III
Tp · Tp · Tp · Tp

Med Sqn — HQ 2 Pz Kw IV

Each 4 Pz Kw IV
Tp · Tp

Strength:

Bn	.....	...	1,014 all ranks
Workshop coy	...	...	136 (approx)
Total tanks	...		69

Fire-power:

LMGs	...	...	...	140
MMGs	...	...	...	8
2-cm (·79-in) tk gun	...		...	7
5-cm (1·97-in) long tk gun	...			27
7·5-cm (2·95-in) long tk gun	...			10
7·5-cm (2·95-in) short tk gun	...			25

NOTES.—(i) It is not certain whether the third lt sqn is included in all battalions.

(ii) *Fire-power* : In the light of Libyan experience, it has been assumed that all Pz Kw IV will be armed with long 7·5-cm (2·95-in) tank guns; approx 50 per cent of Pz Kw III with short 7·5-cm (2·95-in) tank guns, and approx 50 per cent with long 5-cm (1·97-in) tank guns.

(iii) *Probable re-equipment* : The re-equipment of the tk bn in the mot div with the new " Panther " tank is to be expected.

ARTILLERY REGIMENT IN A MOTORIZED DIVISION

TABLE 13

HQ

HQ Tp — Sig Sec — Met Sec — Map Printing Sec

I Fd Bty — II Fd Bty — III Med Bty — IV AA Bty

I Fd Bty / II Fd Bty:
Bty HQ — HQ Tp — Sig Sec
Troop · Troop · Troop — Each four 10·5-cm (4·14-in) gun-hows, 2 LMGs
Lt Arty Coln
Survey Sec

III Med Bty:
Bty HQ — HQ Tp — Sig Sec — Survey Sec
Troop · Troop · Troop — Each four 15-cm (5·91-in) hows, 2 LMGs
Lt Arty Coln

IV AA Bty:
HQ
Hy Tp · Hy Tp — Each four 8·8-cm (3·46-in) AA/A tk guns three 2-cm (·79-in) AA/A tk guns
Lt Tp — Twelve 2-cm (·79-in) SP AA/A tk guns 4 LMGs

Strength : 2,545 all ranks
Fire-power :

LMGs	22
2-cm (·79-in) AA/A tk guns ...	18
8·8-cm (3·46-in) AA/A tk guns	8
10·5-cm (4·14-in) gun-hows	24
15-cm (5·91-in) hows ...	12

TABLE 14

ANTI-TANK BATTALION IN A MOTORIZED DIVISION

HQ

Sig Pl   A tk Coy   A tk Coy   A tk Coy   A tk Coy

HQ   Pl   Pl   Pl

HQ   A tk Sec   A tk Sec   A tk Sec   LMG Sec
2 LMGs

A tk Sec

Each one 5-cm (1·97-in) or 7·5-cm (2·95-in) A tk gun

Strength: 550 all ranks.
Fire-power: 5-cm (1·97-in) or 7·5-cm (2·95-in) A tk guns 27
LMGs 18

NOTES.— (i) The third A tk coy is in some cases replaced by an AA coy with three platoons each of four 2-cm (·79-in) AA/A tk guns SP and 1 LMG.

(ii) Battalions may have one or more SP companies, equipped with 7·5-cm (2·95-in) or 7·62-cm (2·99-in) A tk guns on Pz Kw II or Pz Kw 38 (t) chassis.

MECHANIZED ENGINEER BATTALION IN A MOTORIZED DIVISION   TABLE 15

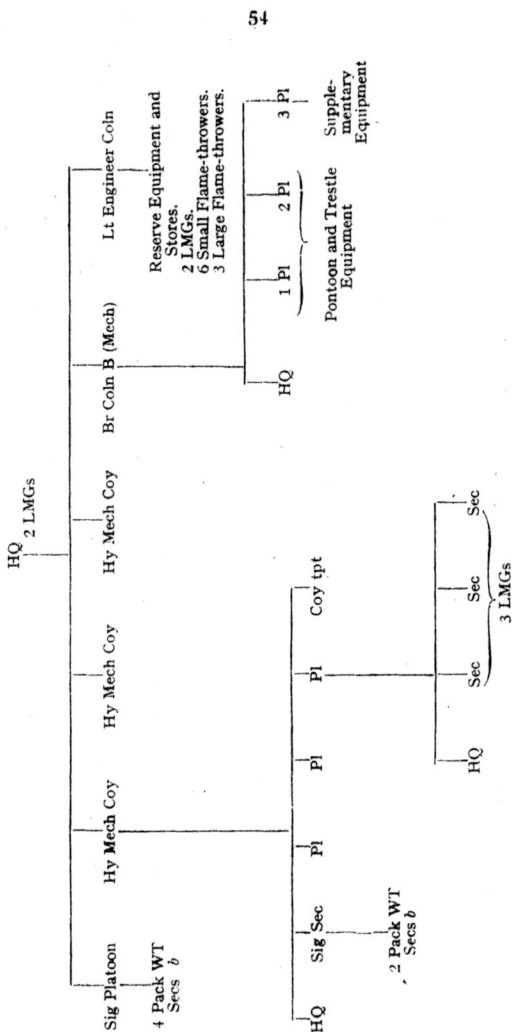

HQ
2 LMGs

Sig Platoon   Hy Mech Coy   Hy Mech Coy   Hy Mech Coy   Br Coln B (Mech)   Lt Engineer Coln

4 Pack WT
Secs *b*

HQ   Sig Sec   Pl   Pl   Pl   Coy tpt

, 2 Pack WT
  Secs *b*

HQ   Sec   Sec   Sec
            3 LMGs

Reserve Equipment and
Stores.
2 LMGs.
6 Small Flame-throwers.
3 Large Flame-throwers.

HQ   1 Pl   2 Pl   3 Pl

Pontoon and Trestle   Supple-
Equipment   mentary
                     Equipment

Strength: 851
Fire-power: LMGs: 31

TABLE 16

SERVICES OF A MOTORIZED DIVISION

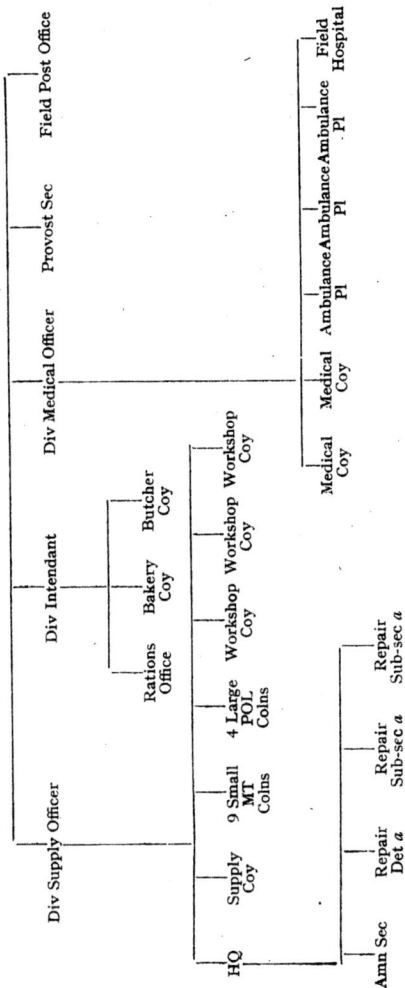

Top level branches:
- Div Supply Officer
- Div Intendant
- Div Medical Officer
- Provost Sec
- Field Post Office

Under Div Supply Officer:
- HQ
- Supply Coy
  - 9 Small MT Colns
  - 4 Large POL Colns
- Workshop Coy
- Amn Sec
  - Repair Det *a*
  - Repair Sub-sec *a*
  - Repair Sub-sec *a*

Under Div Intendant:
- Rations Office
- Bakery Coy
- Butcher Coy
- Workshop Coy
- Workshop Coy

Under Div Medical Officer:
- Medical Coy
  - Medical Coy
  - Ambulance Pl
  - Ambulance Pl
  - Ambulance Pl
  - Field Hospital

Strength: 2,162 all ranks.
Fire-power: 33 LMGs.

NOTES: (i) The armament of the services for local defence varies considerably. 33 LMGs is a typical allotment for services organized as above. A certain number of 2-cm (·79-in) AA/A tk guns may also be included.

(ii) The services under divisional supply officer include an estimated proportionate increase consistent with the inclusion in the division of the tank battalion and the AA Bty.

Divisional HQ

Services

Eng Bn

A tk Bn

Arty Regt

Mot Inf Regt

Mot Inf Regt

Tank Bn

Armd Recce Unit

Sigs Bn

HQ
2 LMGs

Tpt

A tk Coy
or
AA Coy with
twelve 2-cm
('79-in)
AA/A tk guns
(SP)
4 LMGs

A tk Coy

A tk Coy

Hy Mech Coy

Hy Mech Coy

Hy Mech Coy

Hy Mech Coy

Lt Engr
Coln

Reser
Equipmer
Stor
2 LM

Br Coln B

HQ

Sigs Pl

Pl

Pl

Pl

Pl

Each three 5-cm (1·97-in) A tk guns
2 LMGs

Tpt

HQ

Sigs Pl

Pl

Pl

Pl

Pl

Each 3 LMGs

Sigs Pl

IV AA B

III Med Bty

II Fd Bty

I Fd Bty

I Fd Bty

Amn C

HQ

Lt Arty
Coln

Lt Arty
Coln

Lt Inf Coln

Hy Tp

Hy Tp

Lt Tp

HQ Tp

Tp

Tp

Tp

Each four 15-cm (5·91-in)
hows
2 LMGs

Tp

Tp

Tp

Each four 10·5-cm (4·14-in)
gun hows
2 LMGs

Each four 8·8-cm (3·46-in)
AA/A tk guns
and three 2-cm ('79-in) AA/A tk
guns

twelve 2-cm ('79-in)
AA/A tk guns
(SP)
4 LMGs

HQ Tp

Map
printing
Sec

Met Sec

HQ Tp

Sigs Pl

Survey
Sec

Survey
Sec

Sigs
Pl

HQ

Sigs Pl

Workshop
Unit

Med Sqn

Lt Sqn

Lt Sqn

Lt Sqn

HQ Sqn

14 A tk Coy

13 Inf Gun Coy
six 7·5-cm (2·95-in)
Lt Inf guns
two 15-cm (5·91-in)
Hy Inf guns

III Bn

II Bn

I Bn

Lt Coln
3 LMGs

Hy Coy

Armd
Recce Coy

Armd
Recce Coy

Lt Signalling
Coln
1 LMG

2 WT Coy
8 LMGs

Armd
Car
Sqn
24 LMGs
18 2-cm
('79-in)
guns

Pnr Pl
3 LMGs

Inf gun Pl
two 7·5-cm
(2·95-in)
Inf guns

A tk Pl
three 5-cm (1·97-in)
A tk guns
three 2·8-cm (1·1-in)
A tk guns
2 LMGs

Armd Recce Coy
18 LMGs
4 MMGs
3 A tk rifles
two 8-cm (3-in)
mortars

HQ

Tp

Tp

Each 4 Pz Kw IV

Tp

Tp

Each 5 Pz Kw III

HQ

2 Pz Kw IV

HQ

2 Pz Kw III

HQ

2 Pz Kw III

Lt Tk Tp
'Pz Kw II

Pnr Pl
3 LMGs

MC Pl
4 LMGs

AA Pl
8 MGs

Pnr Pl
MC DR Pl
(3 LMGs)

5 Rifle
Coy

6 Rifle
Coy

7 Rifle
Coy

8 MG Coy
12 MMGs
six 8-cm (3-in)
mortars

Each 12 LMGs
three 5-cm (2-in) mortars
3 A tk rifles

Coy

MC Pl
(3 LMGs)

HQ

Pl

Pl

Pl

Each three 5-cm (1·97-in) A tk guns
2 LMGs

MOTORIZED DIVISION—SUMMARY OF PERSONNEL, AFVs, WEAPONS, AND MT

Personnel	Tanks – Pz Kw IV 7.5-cm (2.95) (short)	Tanks – Pz Kw IV 7.5-cm (2.95-in) (long)	Tanks – Pz Kw III 7.5-cm (2.95-in) (short)	Tanks – Pz Kw III 5-cm (1.97-in) (long)	Tanks – Pz Kw II	Armd Cars Light	Armd Cars Heavy	Small Arms LMG	Small Arms MMG	Small Arms A tk Rifles	AA/A tk – 2-cm (.79-in) A tk	AA/A tk – 2-cm (.79-in) AA/A tk	AA/A tk – 2.8-cm (1.1-in) A tk	AA/A tk – 5-cm (1.97-in) (long) tank gun	AA/A tk – 5-cm (1.97-in) A tk	AA/A tk – 7.5-cm (2.95-in) (long) tank gun	AA/A tk – 8.8-cm (3.46-in) AA/A tk guns	Mortars 5-cm (2-in)	Mortars 8-cm (3-in)	CS Arty 7.5-cm (2.95-in) (short) tank guns	CS Arty 7.5-cm (2.95-in) infantry guns	CS Arty 15-cm (5.91-in) infantry guns	Div Arty 10.5-cm (4.14-in) gun-hows	Div Arty 15-cm (5.91-in) hows	MT MV	MT M
181	—	—	—	—	—	—	—	—	2	—	—	—	—	—	—	—	—	—	—	—	—	—	—	—	30	35
456	—	—	—	—	—	—	—	17	—	—	—	—	—	—	—	—	—	—	—	—	—	—	—	—	107	3:
1,140 (Unit qn.)	—	—	—	—	—	18	6	88	12	9	6	12	3	—	3	—	—	—	6	—	2	—	—	—	236	15:
1,014	—	10	25	27	7	—	—	140	8	—	7	—	—	27	18	10	—	—	—	25	—	—	—	—	98	5:
6,200 (Regts)	—	—	—	—	—	—	—	240	72	54	—	18	—	—	18	—	—	54	36	—	12	4	—	—	870	51:
2,545	—	—	—	—	—	—	—	22	—	—	—	—	—	—	27 (18)	—	8	—	—	—	—	—	24	12	500	20:
550	—	—	—	—	—	—	—	18 (16)	—	—	—	(12)	—	—	—	—	—	—	—	—	—	—	—	—	95	4:
851	—	—	—	—	—	—	—	31	—	—	—	—	—	—	—	—	—	—	—	—	—	—	—	—	131	5:
2,162	—	—	—	—	—	—	—	33	—	—	—	—	—	—	—	—	—	—	—	—	—	—	—	—	442	12:
15,099	—	10	25	27	7	18	6	589 (587)	94	63	13	30 (42)	3	27	48 (39)	10	8	54	42	25	14	4	24	12	2,509	1,21:

—A tk battalion.—A tk bns equipped with 7·5-cm (2·95-in) A tk guns in place of 5-cm (1·97-in) A tk guns will be encountered. Figures in brackets are for a battalion, of which the third coy is an AA coy.

Section 24.—THE LIGHT DIVISION

It is as yet possible to give only a *tentative* organization for light divisions. It appears, however, that they are of two types, here referred to for convenience as Type " A " and Type " B." Type " A " is organized on a mechanized, and Type " B " on a horse-drawn basis.

TYPE " A "—Mechanized

	Strength
Two infantry regiments (each of three bns)	6,200
Arty regt (two fd, one med bty).	1,835
Other divisional units (A tk, signals, engineer, recce)	

Guns : Arty regt 36 (24 fd, 12 med)
Close support 18 (incl 4 × 6-in) .
A tk : 69

Mortars : 96 (54 × 2-in ; 42 × 3-in)

Total strength : 13,000 all ranks	
MV ... ... ?	
MC ... ... ?	
Armd Cars ... 24	

NOTE.—It is believed that in light divs of Type " A " div units are mechanized throughout, while the inf regts are transported by troop-carrying MT regts from the GHQ pool.

TYPE " B "—Horse-drawn

	Strength
Two infantry regiments (each of three bns)	6,200
Arty regt (two fd, one med bty)	1,835
Other divisional units (A tk, signals, engineer, recce).	

Guns : Arty regt 36 (24 fd, 12 med)
    Close support 14
    A tk : 72.

Mortars : 130? (60×2-in, 42×3-in, 28?×4-in)

Total strength : 13,000 all ranks.

MV	...	...	?
MC	...	...	?
Armd cars	...	3

NOTE.—Light divisions of Type " B " are at least in part trained and organized for mtn warfare. The allotment of weapons will, therefore, depend to some extent on the country over which they are fighting.

CHAPTER 3

SECTION 25.—**ARMOURED DIVISION**

The armoured division consists of :—

The table facing page 66 shows the organization of the armoured division in outline ; and a summary of personnel, AFVs, weapons, and MT, in the armoured division is given in the table on the reverse.

NOTE.—In some armoured divisions the Panzer Grenadier brigade HQ is not included, and the two Panzer Grenadier regiments are directly under divisional HQ.

SIGNALS BATTALION IN AN ARMOURED DIVISION   TABLE **18**

Bn HQ

Armoured Telephone Coy

Armoured WT Coy   Light Signalling Column *a* (mech)

No. 1 Platoon

No. 2 Platoon   No. 3 Platoon   Transport

HQ

1 Petrol lorry
1 MT repair equip-
ment lorry
1 WT equipment
lorry
2 Tele equipment
lorries
1 Field kitchen
lorry
1 Personnel lorry
3 Signal vehicles
1 LMG.

Med armd WT Sec *b*   Tele-operating Sec *a*   Lt tele Sec *b*   Lt tele Sec *b*   Hy tele Sec *b*   HQ   HQ

Hy tele Sec *b*   Hy tele Sec *b*   Hy tele Sec *b*   Hy tele Sec *b*

Lt armd WT Sec *d*   Lt armd WT Sec *d*   Lt armd WT Sec *d*   Lt armd WT Sec *d*   Med armd WT Sec *b*   Tele-operating Sec *a*   Hy tele Sec *b*   Lt tele Sec *b*   Lt tele Sec *b*   Lt tele Sec *b*   Lt tele Sec *b*

No. 1 Platoon   No. 2 Platoon   No. 3 Platoon   Transport

HQ

HQ   HQ

Lt armd WT Sec *c*   3 armd comd vehicles

Med armd WT Sec *b*   Med armd WT Sec *b*   Med armd WT Sec *b*   Med armd WT Sec *b*   Med armd WT Sec *b*   Med armd WT Sec *b*

Lt armd WT sub-sec *c*   Lt armd WT sub-sec *d*   Lt armd WT sub-sec *d*   Lt armd WT sub-sec *d*   Lt armd WT sub-sec *d*   Lt armd WT sub-sec *d*   Lt armd WT sub-sec *d*

STRENGTH

	Personnel	MC	MT	LMGs
Bn HQ	40	3	10	—
Armoured Tele Coy ...	159	10	38	6
Armoured WT Coy ...	165	14	40	16
Light Sig Coln *a* ...	36	1	9	1
TOTAL	400	28	97 (i)	23

(i) Includes 27 armoured vehicles—Tele Coy 6, WT Coy 21.

HQ (2 LMGs)

Sig Pl   Armd C Sqn   Armd Recce Coy   Armd Recce Coy   Armd Recce Coy   Hy Coy   Lt Coln (3 LMGs)

HQ

Lt Tele-phone Sec *c* (mech)   2 Pack WT Secs (mech)   Lt Armd WT Sec *c* (mech)   3 Med Armd WT Secs *b* (mech)   4 Lt Armd WT Secs *d* (mech)

A tk Pl
Three 5-cm (1·97-in) A tk guns
Three 2·8-cm (1·1-in) A tk guns
2 LMGs

Lt Inf Gun Pl
Two 7·5-cm (2·95-in) inf guns

Pnr Pl
3 LMGs

HQ   Hy Tp   Lt Tp   Lt Tp   Lt Tp

Sec   Sec   Sec   Sec   Sec

Each 2 hy armd cars   Each 3 lt armd cars

HQ   Pl   Pl   Pl   Hy Pl

HQ   Sec   Sec   Sec   HQ   MMG Sec   MMG Sec   Med Mortar Sec

1 A tk rifle   Each 2 LMGs   Each 2 MMGs   Two 8-cm (3-in) mortars

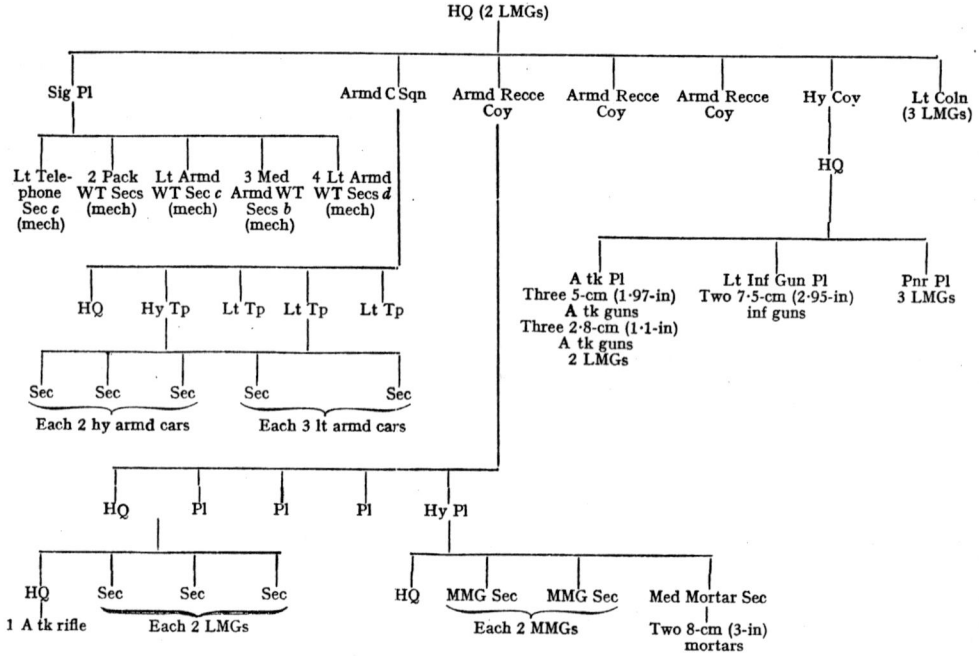

Strength : 1,140 all ranks.

Fire-power :

LMGs	...	...	...	...	...	88
MMGs	...	...	...	...	...	12
A tk rifles	...	...	...	...	...	9
2·8-cm (1·1-in) A tk guns	...	...	...	...	3
5-cm (1·97-in) A tk guns	...	...	...	...	3
8-cm (3-in) mortars	...	...	...	...	6
7·5-cm (2·95-in) inf guns	...	...	...	2
2-cm (·79-in) guns	...	...	...	...	18
or						
2-cm (·79-in) guns	...	...	...	...	12 and
7·5-cm (2·95-in) tk guns	...	...	...	6

NOTES.— (i) *Armd C Sqn.*—The allotment of the various types of armoured cars is not fixed. The following is the allotment upon which the fire-power shown is based :—

6 hy armd cars each with one 2-cm (·79-in) A tk or 7·5-cm (2·95-in) tk gun and 1 LMG.
6 lt armd cars with WT and 1 LMG.
12 lt armd cars with one 2-cm (·79-in) AA/A tk gun and 1 LMG.

(ii) *Fire-power.*—The fire-power shown for the unit is based on the assumption that all three armd recce coys are transported in " Volkswagen " or on MC. For each armd recce coy transported in armd carriers, the fire-power shown will probably be increased by three 3·7-cm (1·45-in) A tk guns and 16 LMGs.

TANK REGIMENT IN AN ARMOURED DIVISION TABLE 20

Regt HQ

HQ Sqn — Bn — Bn — Bn — Lt AA Coy — Workshop Coy

Twelve 2-cm (·79-in)
AA/A tk guns
4 LMGs

Sigs Pl — Lt Tank Tp

1 Pz Kw III
2 Hy ACV

7 Pz Kw II

Bn HQ

HQ Sqn — Lt Sqn — Lt Sqn — Med Sqn

Sigs Pl — Lt Tank Tp — Pnr Pl (3 LMGs) — MC Pl (4 LMGs) — AA Pl (8 MGs)

7 Pz Kw II

1 Pz Kw III
2 Hy ACV

HQ — Tp — Tp

2 Pz Kw IV — Each 4 Pz Kw IV

HQ — Tp — Tp — Tp

2 Pz Kw III — Each 5 Pz Kw III

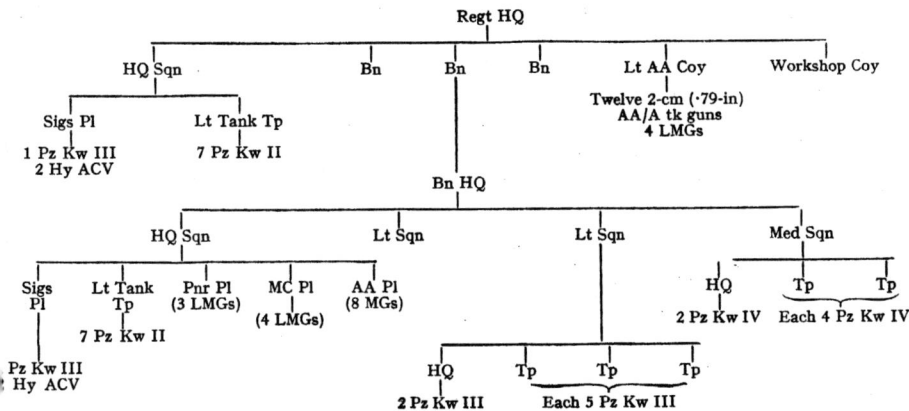

Strength :				Tanks :				Fire-power :						
Regt	...	...	2,745 all ranks	Pz Kw II	...	...	28	LMGs	...	...	...	...	...	333
Bn HQ }	...	...	256	Pz Kw III	...	...	106	MMGs	...	...	...	...	...	24
HQ Sqn }				Pz Kw IV	...	...	30	2-cm (·79-in) tk guns	...	...	...	28
Lt Sqn	...	...	152				—	2-cm (·79-in) AA/A tk guns...	...	...	12
Med Sqn	...	...	136	Total	...	...	164	5-cm (1·97-in) long tk guns	...	...	50
Workshop unit	...	...	251					7·5-cm (2·95-in) long tk guns	...	...	30
Lt AA Coy	...	...	180					7·5-cm (2·95-in) short tk guns	...	...	56

NOTES : (i) While the tk regt of 3 bns each of 3 sqns is regarded as normal, tk regts of 2 bns with 3 or 4 sqns each will also be encountered.

(ii) *Fire-power.*—In the light of Libyan experience it has been assumed that all Pz Kw IV will be armed with long 7·5-cm (2·95-in) tank guns, approx 50 per cent of Pz Kw III with short 7·5-cm (2·95-in) tank guns, and approx 50 per cent with long 5-cm (1·97-in) tk guns.

(iii) *Probable re-equipment.*—It is believed that one of the bns in the regt will be reorganized as a heavy tk bn equipped with Pz Kw VI (Tiger) tks. The appearance of the new " Panther " tk in tk regiments is also to be expected.

(a) *Organization*

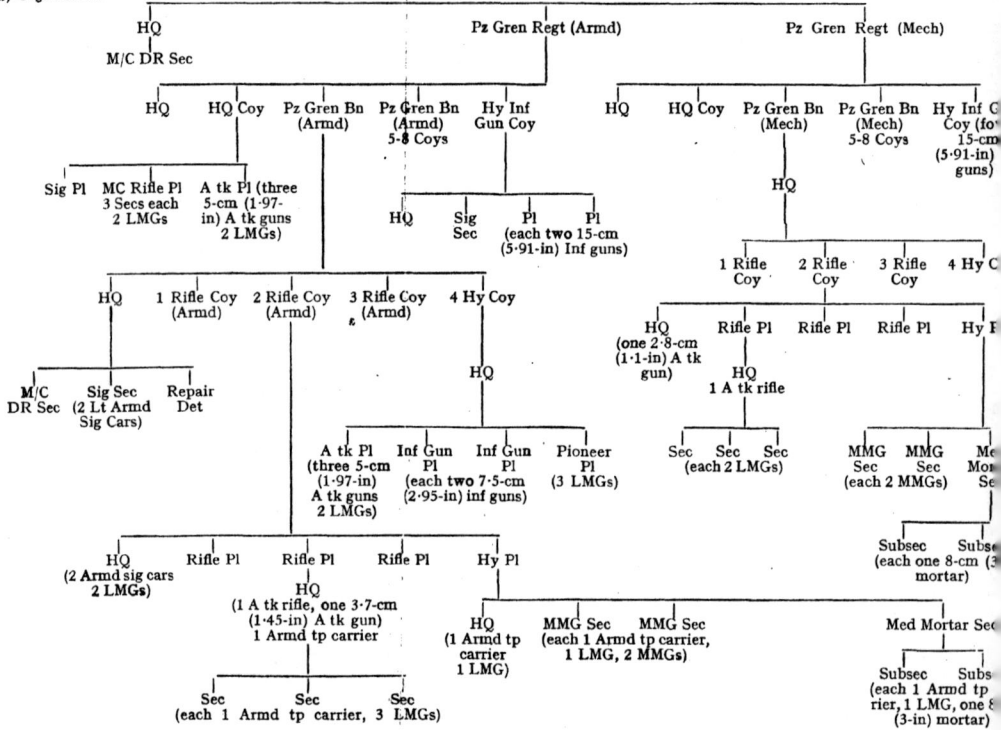

HQ
M/C DR Sec

Pz Gren Regt (Armd)

Pz Gren Regt (Mech)

Pz Gren Regt (Armd):

HQ — HQ Coy — Pz Gren Bn (Armd) — Pz Gren Bn (Armd) 5-8 Coys — Hy Inf Gun Coy

HQ Coy:
- Sig Pl — 3 Secs each 2 LMGs
- MC Rifle Pl 5-cm (1·97-in) A tk guns 2 LMGs
- A tk Pl (three 5-cm (1·97-in) A tk guns 2 LMGs)

Hy Inf Gun Coy:
- HQ — Sig Sec — Pl (each **two** 15-cm (5·91-in) Inf guns) — Pl

Pz Gren Bn (Armd):
HQ — 1 Rifle Coy (Armd) — 2 Rifle Coy (Armd) — 3 Rifle Coy (Armd) — 4 Hy Coy

HQ (Bn):
- M/C DR Sec — Sig Sec (2 Lt Armd Sig Cars) — Repair Det

3 Rifle Coy (Armd):
HQ

4 Hy Coy:
HQ — A tk Pl (three 5-cm (1·97-in) A tk guns 2 LMGs) — Inf Gun Pl — Inf Gun Pl (each **two** 7·5-cm (2·95-in) inf guns) — Pioneer Pl (3 LMGs)

Rifle Coy:
HQ (2 Armd sig cars 2 LMGs) — Rifle Pl — Rifle Pl — Rifle Pl — Hy Pl

Rifle Pl:
HQ (1 A tk rifle, one 3·7-cm (1·45-in) A tk gun) 1 Armd tp carrier — Sec — Sec — Sec (each 1 Armd tp carrier, 3 LMGs)

Hy Pl:
HQ (1 Armd tp carrier 1 LMG) — MMG Sec — MMG Sec (each 1 Armd tp carrier, 1 LMG, 2 MMGs)

Pz Gren Regt (Mech):

HQ — HQ Coy — Pz Gren Bn (Mech) — Pz Gren Bn (Mech) 5-8 Coys — Hy Inf Coy (for 15-cm (5·91-in) guns)

Pz Gren Bn (Mech):
HQ — 1 Rifle Coy — 2 Rifle Coy — 3 Rifle Coy — 4 Hy Coy

Rifle Coy:
HQ (one 2·8-cm (1·1-in) A tk gun) — Rifle Pl — Rifle Pl — Rifle Pl — Hy Pl

Rifle Pl:
HQ 1 A tk rifle — Sec — Sec — Sec (each 2 LMGs)

Hy Coy:
MMG Sec — MMG Sec (each 2 MMGs) — Mortar Sec

Mortar Sec:
Subsec — Subsec (each one 8-cm (3-in) mortar)

Med Mortar Sec:
Subsec — Subsec (each 1 Armd tp carrier, 1 LMG, one 8-cm (3-in) mortar)

NOTES : (i) There is no fixed allotment of armd and mech coys to a Pz Gren bde. The bde shown above is assumed to have one regt armd throughout and one regt mech throughout. The strength and fire-power of the bde will vary according to the actual allotment of armd coys.

(ii) Hy coys in armd Pz Gren bns may be issued with hy projectors on the rocket principle, but the scale of allotment is not known.

(b) *Strength and Fire-Power*

PANZER GRENADIER BRIGADE

PERSONNEL	Bde Total	Bde HQ	Regt (armd)	Regt HQ	Regt HQ Coy	Hy Inf Gun Coy	Pz Gren Bn (armd)	Bn HQ (armd)	Pz Gren Coy (armd)	Hy Coy	Regt (mech)	Bn (mech)	Bn HQ (mech)	Pz Gren Coy (mech)
Offrs ...	142	4	72	3	6	3	30	7	6	5	66	27	7	5
ORs ...	4,256	38	2,061	13	178	104	883	101	206	164	2,157	931	98	223
Total ...	4,398	42	2,133	16	184	107	913	108	212	169	2,223	958	105	228
FIRE-POWER														
Rifles ...	2,752	32	1,330	11	89	80	575	77	128	114	1,390	605	74	139
Pistols ...	1,341	7	652	3	85	24	270	29	65	46	682	285	29	70
Small Arms — Machine Carbines	431	3	271	2	12	3	127	4	38	9	157	70	4	19
A tk Rifles ...	36	—	18	—	—	—	9	—	3	—	18	9	—	3
LMGs ...	348	—	222	—	8	—	107	—	34	5	126	59	—	18
MMGs ...	48	—	24	—	—	—	12	—	4	—	24	12	—	4
Mortars 8-cm (3-in) ...	24	—	12	—	—	—	6	—	2	—	12	6	—	2
A tk Guns 2·8-cm (1·1-in) ...	6	—	—	—	—	—	—	—	—	—	6	3	—	1
3·7-cm (1·45-in) ...	18	—	18	—	—	—	9	—	3	—	—	—	—	—
5-cm (1·97-in) ...	18	—	9	—	3	—	3	—	—	3	9	3	—	—
Inf Guns 7·5-cm (2·95-in) ...	16	—	8	—	—	—	4	—	—	4	8	4	—	—
15-cm (5·91-in) ...	8	—	4	—	—	4	—	—	—	—	4	—	—	—

ARTILLERY REGIMENT IN AN ARMOURED DIVISION

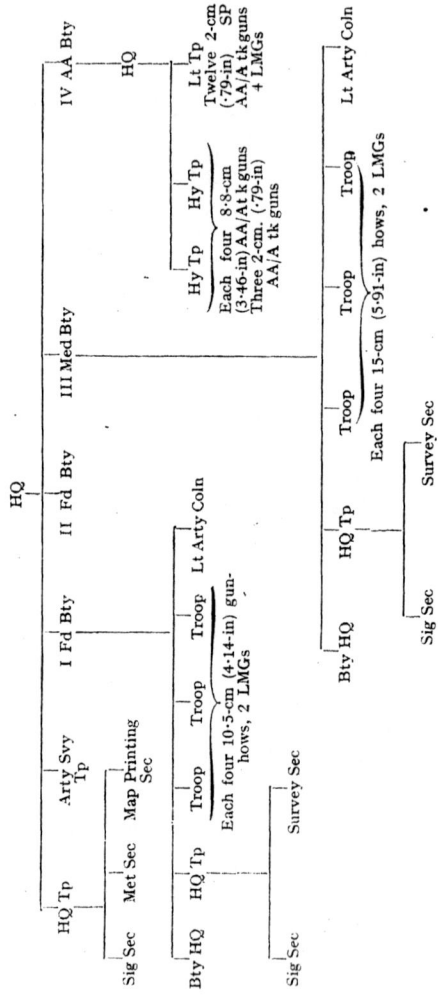

TABLE 21A

HQ

HQ Tp — Arty Svy Tp — I Fd Bty — II Fd Bty — III Med Bty — IV AA Bty

Sig Sec — Met Sec — Map Printing Sec

Bty HQ — HQ Tp — Troop — Troop — Troop — Lt Arty Coln

Each four 10·5-cm (4·14-in) gun-hows, 2 LMGs

Sig Sec — Survey Sec

HY Tp — Hy Tp — Hy Tp

Each four 8·8-cm (3·46-in) AA/A tk guns
Three 2-cm. (·79-in) AA/A tk guns

HQ

Lt Tp
Twelve 2-cm (·79-in) SP AA/A tk guns + LMGs

Bty HQ — HQ Tp — Troop — Troop — Troop — Lt Arty Coln

Each four 15-cm (5·91-in) hows, 2 LMGs

Sig Sec — Survey Sec

NOTES : (i) Regiments may have one or more field btys, equipped with SP guns.
(ii) Regiments may include a troop of six or eight 15-cm (5·91-in) smoke mortars 41.

Strength : 2,812 all ranks.
Fire-power :
LMGs	...	22
2-cm (·79-in) AA/A tk guns ...	...	18
8·8-cm (3·46-in) AA/A tk guns	...	8
10·5-cm (4·14-in) gun-hows ...	...	24
15-cm (5·91-in) hows	...	12

TABLE 21B

ASSAULT GUN BTY IN AN ARMOURED DIVISION

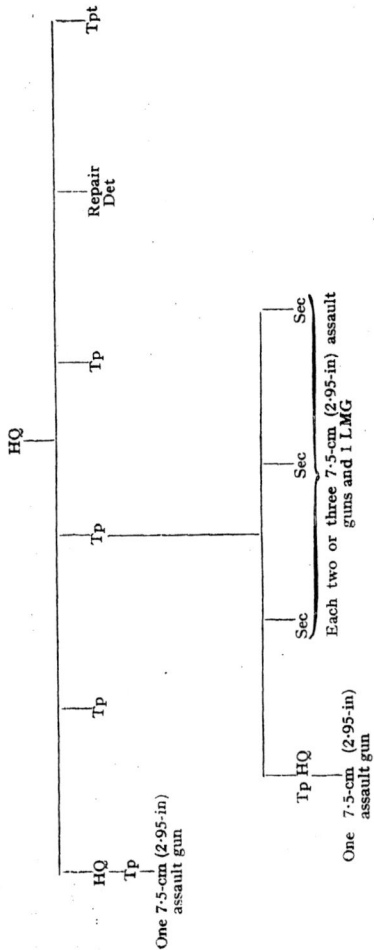

HQ

```
HQ          Tp        Tp        Tp         Repair      Tpt
 |                               |           Det
 Tp                             Sec  Sec  Sec
```

One 7·5-cm (2·95-in)
assault gun

Tp HQ

One 7·5-cm (2·95-in)
assault gun

Each two or three 7·5-cm (2·95-in) assault
guns and 1 LMG

Strength : (lower establishment) 450 all ranks.
Fire-power : 7·5-cm (2·95-in) assault guns   22 or 31
      LMGs   9
MT :   Mot vehicles (lower establishment) 130
      MCs   41

TABLE 22

ANTI-TANK BATTALION IN AN ARMOURED DIVISION

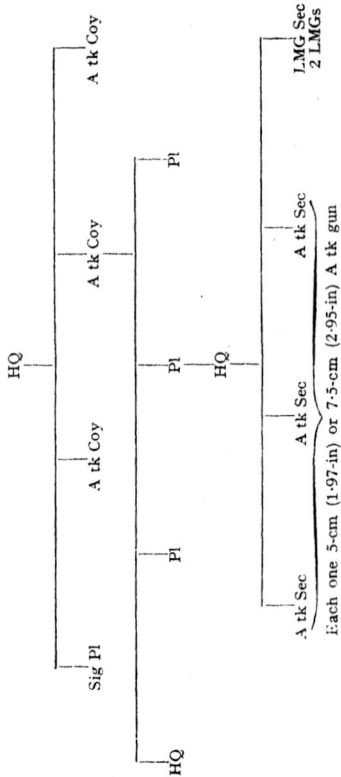

Organisation chart:

HQ — Sig Pl — A tk Coy — A tk Coy — A tk Coy

A tk Coy: HQ — Pl — Pl — Pl

Pl: HQ — A tk Sec — A tk Sec — A tk Sec — LMG Sec (2 LMGs)

A tk Sec: Each one 5-cm (1·97-in) or 7·5-cm (2·95-in) A tk gun

Strength : 550 all ranks.

Fire-power : 5-cm (1·97-in) or 7·5-cm (2·95-in) A tk guns ... 27
LMGs 18

NOTES : (i) The third A tk coy is in some cases replaced by an AA coy with three platoons each of four 2-cm (·79-in) AA/A tk guns SP and 1 LMG.

(ii) Battalions may have one or more SP companies, equipped with 7·5-cm (2·95-in) or 7·62-cm (2·99-in) A tk guns on Pz Kw II or Pz Kw 38 (t) chassis.

TABLE 23

ARMOURED ENGINEER BATTALION IN AN ARMOURED DIVISION

HQ
2 LMGs

Sig Pl — 4 pack WT sections b

Lt mech Coy — HQ — Sig Pl — 2 pack WT sections b — Pl — Pl — Pl — HQ — Sec. — Sec. — Sec. — 3 LMGs

Lt mech Coy

Armd eng Coy — HQ — 1 armd sig car — Sig Pl — 2 pack WT secs b — Hy eng pl — HQ — 6 armd tp carriers 4 LMGs — Sec — Sec — Sec — Lt eng pl — Lt eng pl — Lt eng pl — HQ — Sec — Sec — Sec — 3 LMGs

Bridging Coln K — HQ — 1 Pl — 2 Pl — Pontoon and trestle equipment — 3 Pl — 4 Pl — Tank bridge-laying platoon — 1 Pz Kw II — 4 Pz Kw IV — 5 LMGs — One 2-cm (·79-in) A tk gun — Supplementary bridging equipment

Lt eng coln — Reserve equipment and stores — 2 LMGs — 6 small flame-throwers — 3 med flame-throwers

Strength: 898 all ranks.
Fire-power :
LMGs 37
2-cm (·79-in) A tk gun ... 1

NOTE.—In place of Br Coln K some battalions may still have Br Coln B. Some armd divs now have 2 br colns, either 2 K or 1 K and 1 B. It is not known in how many bns a tk bridge-laying platoon has been formed.

SERVICES OF AN ARMOURED DIVISION

TABLE 24

Div supply officer

Div Intendant — Rations office | Bakery coy | Butcher coy

Div Medical officer

Provost Sec

Field Post Office

Medical coy | Medical coy | Ambulance Pl | Ambulance Pl | Ambulance Pl | Ambulance Pl

HQ — Supply coy | 9 small MT colns | 6 large POL colns | Workshop coy | Workshop coy | Workshop coy | Workshop coy | Workshop coy

Amn sec — Repair det *a* | Repair sub-sec *a* | Repair sub-sec *a*

Strength: 2,326 all ranks.
Fire-power: 35 LMGs.

Note.—The armament of the services for local defence varies considerably. 35 LMGs is a typical allotment for services organized as above. A certain number of 2-cm (·79-in) AA/A tk guns may also be included.

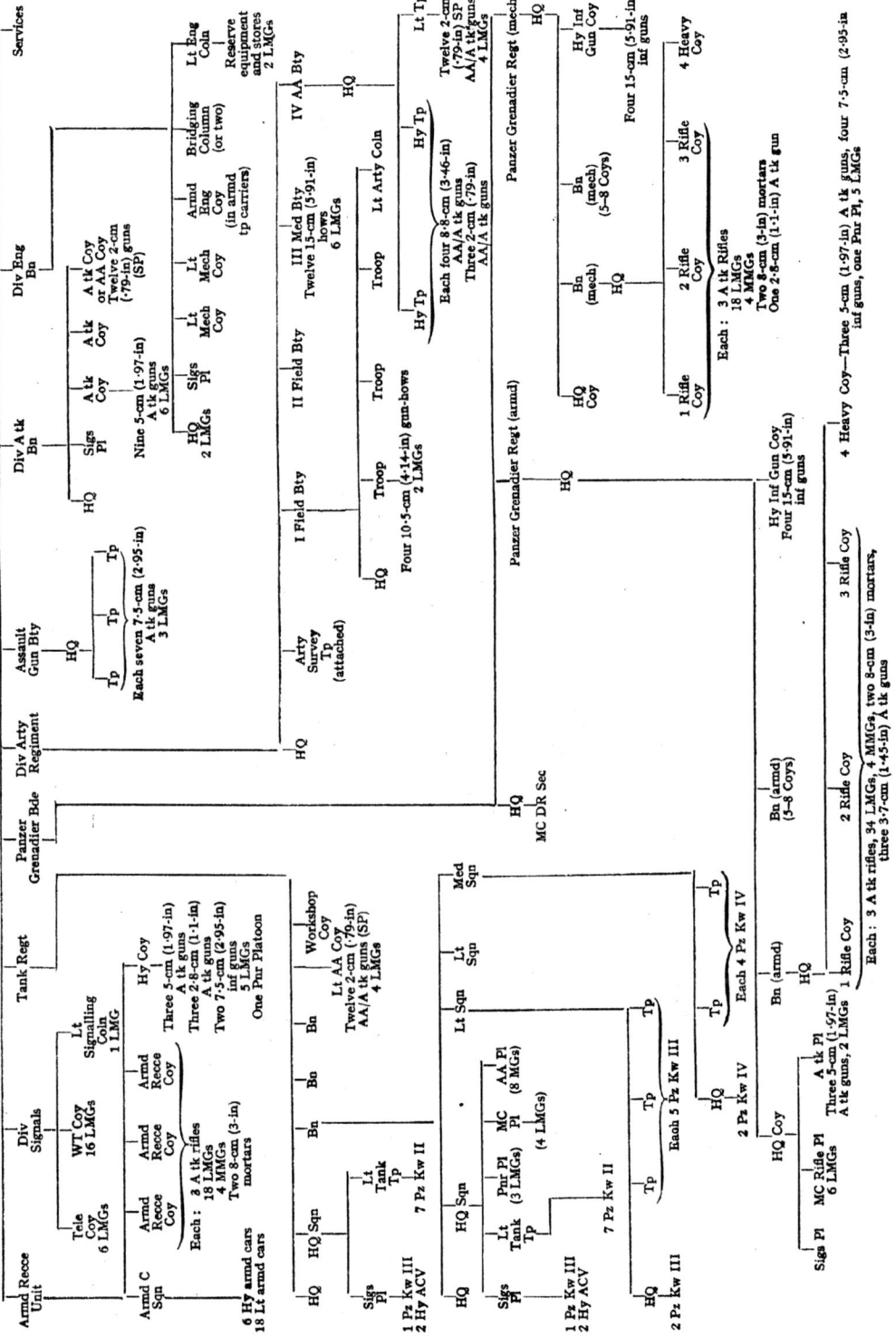

Services

Div Eng Bn
- Lt Eng Coin — Reserve equipment and stores 2 LMGs
- Bridging Column (or two)
- Armd Eng Coy (in armd tp carriers)
- Lt Mech Coy
- Lt Mech Coy
- A tk Coy or AA Coy — Twelve 2-cm (·79-in) guns (SP)
- HQ
- Sigs Pl

Div A tk Bn
- A tk Coy — Nine 5-cm (1·97-in) A tk guns 6 LMGs
- Sigs Pl
- HQ 2 LMGs

Assault Gun Bty
- HQ
- Tp
- Tp
- Tp
- Each seven 7·5-cm (2·95-in) A tk guns 3 LMGs

Div Arty Regiment
- HQ
- Arty Survey Tp (attached)
- I Field Bty — Four 10·5-cm (4·14-in) gun-hows 2 LMGs
  - Troop
  - Troop
  - Troop
- II Field Bty
  - Troop
  - Troop
- III Med Bty — Twelve 15-cm (5·91-in) hows 6 LMGs
  - Troop
  - Troop
- IV AA Bty — Twelve 2-cm (·79-in) SP AA/A tk guns 4 LMGs
  - HQ
  - Lt Arty Coin
  - Lt Tp
  - Hy Tp — Each four 8·8-cm (3·46-in) AA/A tk guns Three 2-cm (·79-in) AA/A tk guns
  - Hy Tp

Panzer Grenadier Bde
- HQ
- MC DR Sec

Panzer Grenadier Regt (armd)
- HQ
- Hy Inf Gun Coy — Four 15-cm (5·91-in) inf guns
- Bn (armd) (3–8 Coys)
  - HQ
  - 1 Rifle Coy
  - 2 Rifle Coy
  - 3 Rifle Coy — Each: 3 A tk rifles, 34 LMGs, 4 MMGs, two 8-cm (3-in) mortars, three 3·7-cm (1·45-in) A tk guns
- Bn (armd)
  - HQ
  - 1 Rifle Coy
  - 2 Rifle Coy
  - 3 Rifle Coy

Panzer Grenadier Regt (mech)
- HQ
- Hy Inf Gun Coy — Four 15-cm (5·91-in) inf guns
- Heavy Coy
- Bn (mech) (5–8 Coys)
  - HQ
  - 1 Rifle Coy
  - 2 Rifle Coy — Each: 3 A tk rifles 18 LMGs 4 MMGs Two 8-cm (3-in) mortars One 2·8-cm (1·1-in) A tk gun
  - 3 Rifle Coy
- Bn (mech)
  - 4 Heavy Coy—Three 5-cm (1·97-in) A tk guns, four 7·5-cm (2·95-in) inf guns, one Pnr Pl, 5 LMGs

Tank Regt
- HQ
- Sigs Pl — 1 Pz Kw III, 2 Hy ACV
- HQ Sqn
- Lt Tank Tp — 7 Pz Kw II
- Lt Tank Tp
- Sigs Pl — 1 Pz Kw III, 2 Hy ACV
- HQ Sqn
- 7 Pz Kw II
- Hy Coy — Three 5-cm (1·97-in) A tk guns, Three 2·8-cm (1·1-in) A tk guns, Two 7·5-cm (2·95-in) inf guns, 5 LMGs, One Pnr Platoon
- Bn
- Bn
- Bn
- Lt AA Coy — Twelve 2-cm (·79-in) AA/A tk guns (SP) 4 LMGs
- Workshop Coy
- HQ
- Sigs Pl — 2 Pz Kw III
- HQ Coy
  - MC Rifle Pl 6 LMGs
  - Pnr Pl (3 LMGs)
  - MC Pl (4 LMGs)
  - AA Pl (8 MGs)
  - A tk Pl — Three 5-cm A tk guns, 2 LMGs
- Med Sqn
- Lt Sqn
  - HQ
  - Tp
  - Tp — Each 5 Pz Kw III
- Lt Sqn
  - HQ
  - Tp
  - Tp — 2 Pz Kw IV
- Tp
- Tp — Each 4 Pz Kw IV

Div Signals
- Tele Coy 6 LMGs
- WT Coy 16 LMGs

Armd Recce Unit
- Armd C Sqn
  - Armd Recce Coy
  - Armd Recce Coy
  - Armd Recce Coy — Each: 3 A tk rifles 18 LMGs 4 MMGs Two 8-cm (3-in) mortars
  - 6 Hy armd cars 18 Lt armd cars
- Lt Signalling Coin 1 LMG

ARMOURED DIVISION—SUMMARY OF PERSONNEL, AFVs, WEAPONS, AND MT

Unit	Personnel	Pz Kw IV 7·5-cm (2·95-in) long	Pz Kw IV 7·5-cm (2·95-in) short	Pz Kw III 7·5-cm (2·95-in) short	Pz Kw III 5-cm (1·97-in) long	Pz Kw II	Armd Cars Light	Armd Cars Heavy	LMG	MMG	A tk rifles	2-cm (·79-in) A tk	2-cm (·79-in) AA/A tk	2·8-cm (1·1-in) A tk	3·7-cm (1·45-in) A tk	5-cm (1·97-in) long tank guns	5-cm (1·97-in) A tk	7·5-cm (2·95-in) long tank guns	8·8-cm (3·46-in) AA/A tk guns	8-cm (3-in)	7·5-cm (2·95-in) short tank guns	7·5-cm (2·95-in) infantry guns	15-cm (5·91-in) infantry guns	10·5-cm (4·14-in) gun-hows	15-cm (5·91-in) hows	MV	MC
...	185	—	—	—	—	—	—	—	—	2	—	—	—	—	—	—	—	—	—	—	—	—	—	—	—	31	3
: Unit	1,140	—	—	—	—	—	—	6	88	12	9	6	12	3	—	—	3	—	—	6	—	2	—	—	—	236	15
...	2,745	30	—	56	50	28	18	—	333	24	—	28	12	—	—	50	—	30	—	—	56	—	—	—	—	390	17
...	400	—	—	—	—	—	—	—	23	—	—	—	—	—	—	—	—	—	—	—	—	—	—	—	—	97	2
e	4,398	—	—	—	—	—	—	—	348	48	36	—	18	6	18	—	18	—	—	24	—	16	8	—	—	706	30
...	2,812	—	—	—	—	—	—	—	22	—	—	—	—	—	—	—	—	—	—	—	—	—	—	24	12	526	20
i Bty	450	—	—	—	—	—	—	—	10	—	—	—	—	—	—	—	—	22	8	—	—	—	—	—	—	130	4
...	550	—	—	—	—	—	—	—	18 (16)	—	—	—	(12)	—	—	—	27 (18)	—	—	—	—	—	—	—	—	95	4
...	898	—	—	—	—	—	—	—	37	—	—	1	—	—	—	—	—	—	—	—	—	—	—	—	—	178	7
...	2,326	—	—	—	—	—	—	—	35	—	—	—	—	—	—	—	—	—	—	—	—	—	—	—	—	520	13
.	15,904	30	—	56	50	28	18	6	914 (912)	86	45	35	42 (54)	9	18	50	48 (39)	52	8	30	56	18	8	24	12	2,909	119

a.—(i) *Assault Gun Bty* : This unit is NOT included in all divisions.

(ii) *A tk bns* : Bns equipped with 7·5-cm (2·95-in) A tk guns in place of 5-cm (1·97-in) guns will be encountered. Figures in brackets are for a battalion, of which the third company is an AA Coy.

CHAPTER IV

SECTION 26.—MOUNTAIN DIVISION

The mountain division consists of :—

The table **facing page 74** shows the organization of the mountain division in outline, and a summary of personnel and weapons in the mountain division is given on page **75**.

SIGNALS BATTALION IN A MOUNTAIN DIVISION   TABLE 26

Bn HQ (part mech)

No. 1 Coy
Mtn telephone coy
(part mech)

No. 2 Coy   Light Mtn   Carrier coln (thought
Mtn Wireless Sig Coln   to be set up, at need,
Coy (part mech)   from the drivers of
                          the mules in 2 Pl of
                          No. 1 Coy)

1 Platoon   2 Platoon   3 Platoon   Transport

Tele inter-   Mtn tele   Mtn tele   Tele-   Tele-
cept sec   operating   operating   operating operating
(mech)   sec   sec   sec a   sec a

Lt WT   Lt WT   Hy tele   Hy mtn tele Hy mtn tele Hy mtn tele Hy mtn tele Hy mtn tele
sec b   sec b   sec b   sec (mule)   sec (mule)   sec (mule)   sec (mule)   sec (mule)
                  (mech)

1 Platoon   2 Platoon   3 Platoon   Transport

Lt mtn   Lt mtn   Mtn pack   Mtn pack   Mtn pack Mtn pack Mtn pack Mtn pack
WT sec c WT sec c WT sec b   WT sec b   WT sec b WT sec b WT sec b WT sec b

Med   Med   Lt mtn Lt mtn Lt mtn Lt mtn Lt WT   Lt WT   Mtn   Mtn   Mtn   Mtn   Mtn   Mtn   Pack   Cipher
WT   WT   WT   WT   WT   WT   sec a   sec a   pack   pack   pack   pack   pack   pack   WT   sec
sec b sec b sec b   sec b   sec b   sec b   (mech)   (mech)   WT   WT   WT   WT   WT   WT   sec b (mech)
                                                                sec d sec d sec d sec d sec d sec d (mech)

Strength (estimates)

	Personnel	MT	MC	LMGs
Bn HQ	24	5	2	—
Mtn Telephone Coy	195	35	13	10
Mtn Wireless Coy	143	30	12	6
Lt mtn Sig Coln	36	9	2	1
Total	398	79	29	17

TABLE 27

RECONNAISSANCE UNIT IN A MOUNTAIN DIVISION

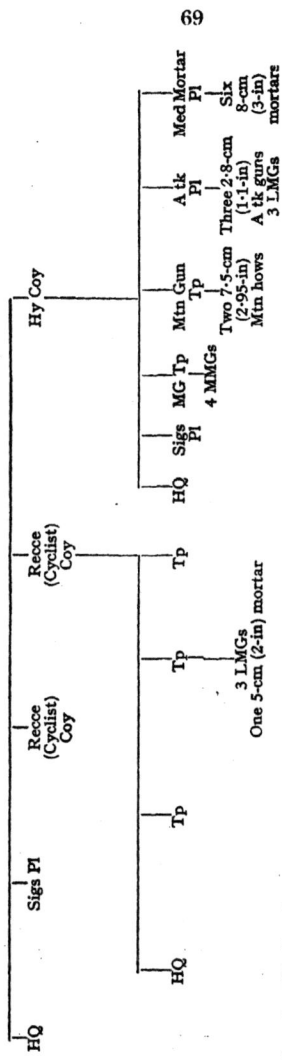

Organization:

HQ — Sigs Pl — Recce (Cyclist) Coy — Recce (Cyclist) Coy — Hy Coy

Recce (Cyclist) Coy: HQ, Tp, Tp, Tp, Tp
3 LMGs
One 5-cm (2-in) mortar

Hy Coy: HQ, Sigs Pl, MG Tp (4 MMGs), Mtn Gun Tp (Two 7·5-cm (2·95-in) Mtn hows), A tk Pl (Three 2·8-cm (1·1-in) A tk guns, 3 LMGs), Med Mortar Pl (Six 8-cm (3-in) mortars)

Strength : 561 all ranks.
Fire-power :
LMGs ...	21
MMGs ...	4
5-cm (2-in) mortars ...	6
8-cm (3-in) mortars ...	6
2·8-cm (1·1-in) A tk guns ...	3
7·5-cm (2·95-in) mtn hows ...	2

NOTE.—It is probable that the six 8-cm (3-in) mortars in the hy coy may be replaced by four 12-cm (4·71-in) mortars.

MOUNTAIN RIFLE REGIMENT IN A MOUNTAIN DIVISION

TABLE 28

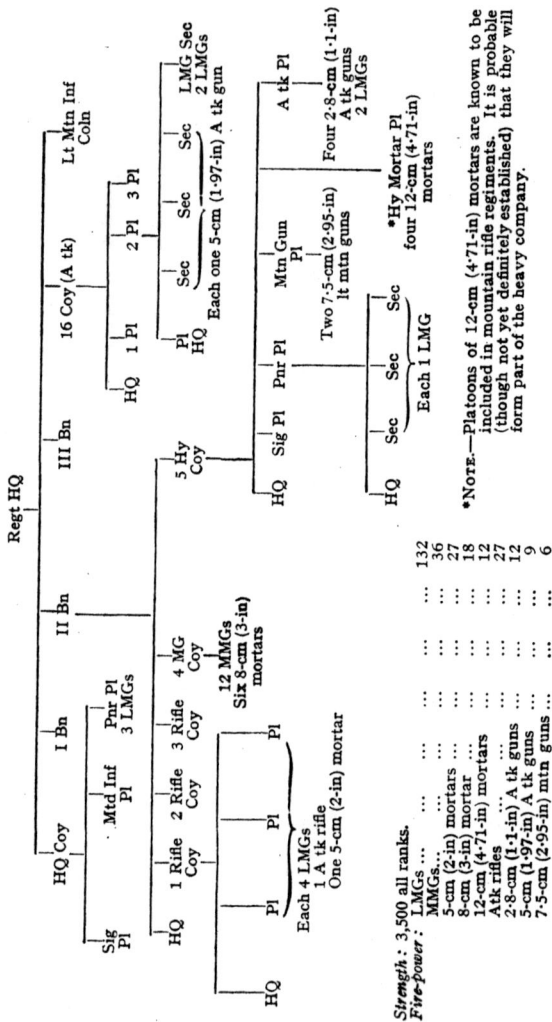

Regt HQ

I Bn — II Bn — III Bn — 16 Coy (A tk) — Lt Mtn Inf Coln

HQ Coy: Sig Pl, Mtd Inf Pl, 1 Rifle Coy, 2 Rifle Coy, Pnr Pl 3 LMGs, 3 Rifle Coy, 4 MG Coy

HQ — 1 Pl — 2 Pl — 3 Pl

HQ: 1 Rifle Coy HQ — Pl — Pl — Pl

Each 4 LMGs
1 A tk rifle
One 5-cm (2-in) mortar

4 MG Coy: 12 MMGs
Six 8-cm (3-in) mortars

16 Coy (A tk): Pl HQ — Sec — Sec — Sec — LMG Sec 2 LMGs
Each one 5-cm (1·97-in) A tk gun

5 Hy Coy: HQ — Sig Pl — Pnr Pl — Mtn Gun Pl — A tk Pl

Mtn Gun Pl: Two 7·5-cm (2·95-in) lt mtn guns

A tk Pl: Four 2·8-cm (1·1-in) A tk guns 2 LMGs

HQ: Sec — Sec — Sec
Each 1 LMG

*Hy Mortar Pl four 12-cm (4·71-in) mortars

*Note.—Platoons of 12-cm (4·71-in) mortars are known to be included in mountain rifle regiments. It is probable (though not yet definitely established) that they will form part of the heavy company.

Strength: 3,500 all ranks.

Fire-power:

LMGs ...	132
MMGs ...	36
5-cm (2-in) mortars	27
8-cm (3-in) mortar	18
12-cm (4·71-in) mortars	12
A tk rifles	27
2·8-cm (1·1-in) A tk guns	12
5-cm (1·97-in) A tk guns	9
7·5-cm (2·95-in) mtn guns	6

TABLE 29

MOUNTAIN ARTILLERY REGIMENT IN A MOUNTAIN DIVISION

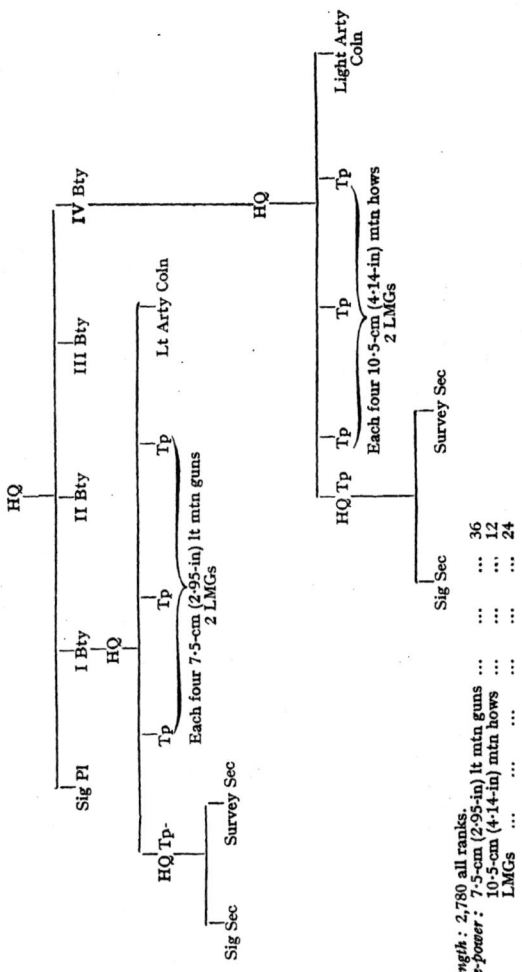

HQ

| Sig Pl | I Bty | II Bty | III Bty | IV Bty |

HQ

Tp Tp

Each four 7·5-cm (2·95-in) lt mtn guns
2 LMGs

Lt Arty Coln

HQ Tp-

Sig Sec | Survey Sec

HQ

HQ Tp | Tp | Tp | Tp | Light Arty Coln

Each four 10·5-cm (4·14-in) mtn hows
2 LMGs

Survey Sec

Sig Sec

Strength: 2,780 all ranks.
Fire-power: 7·5-cm (2·95-in) lt mtn guns 36
10·5-cm (4·14-in) mtn hows 12
LMGs 24

TABLE 30

ANTI-TANK BATTALION IN A MOUNTAIN DIVISION

HQ

Sig Pl — A tk Coy — A tk Coy — A tk Coy

Pl — Pl — Pl — HQ

A tk Sec — A tk Sec — A tk Sec — LMG Sec 2 LMGs

Each one 5-cm (1·97-in) or 7·5-cm (2·95-in) A tk gun

Strength : 550 all ranks.

Fire-power : 5-cm (1·97-in) or 7·5-cm (2·95-in) A tk guns ... 27
LMGs 18

NOTES.— (i) The third A tk Coy is in some cases replaced by an AA Coy with three platoons each of four 2-cm (·79-in) AA/A tk guns SP and 1 LMG.

(ii) It is not known whether companies in the A tk Bn of a Mtn Div will be equipped with SP guns.

MOUNTAIN ENGINEER BATTALION IN A MOUNTAIN DIVISION   TABLE 31

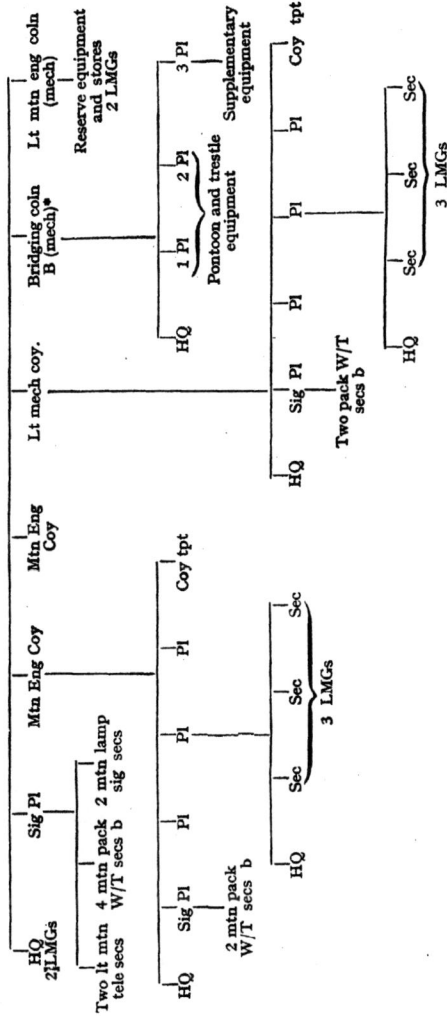

Top level units:

- HQ 2 LMGs
- Sig Pl
  - Two lt mtn tele secs   4 mtn pack W/T secs b   2 mtn lamp sig secs
- Mtn Eng Coy
- Mtn Eng Coy
- Lt mech coy.
- Bridging coln B (mech)*
  - Pontoon and trestle equipment   Supplementary equipment
- Lt mtn eng coln (mech)
  - Reserve equipment and stores 2 LMGs

Mtn Eng Coy breakdown:

- HQ
  - Sig Pl
    - 2 mtn pack W/T secs b
  - Pl
  - Pl (3 LMGs: Sec, Sec, Sec)
  - Pl
  - Coy tpt

Lt mech coy breakdown:

- HQ
  - Sig Pl
    - Two pack W/T secs b
  - Pl
  - Pl
  - Pl
  - Coy tpt
  - (3 LMGs: Sec, Sec, Sec)

Bridging coln B (mech) breakdown:

- HQ
  - 1 Pl   2 Pl   3 Pl

Strength: 1043.
Fire-power: LMGs   29

* Attached when necessary. It is known, however, that a mtn bridging column G exists,
It is of recent formation, but it is not known if it is now part of the mtn div engineer bn.
The mtn bridging coln G has 2 LMGs and 31 mot vehicles.

SERVICES OF A MOUNTAIN DIVISION

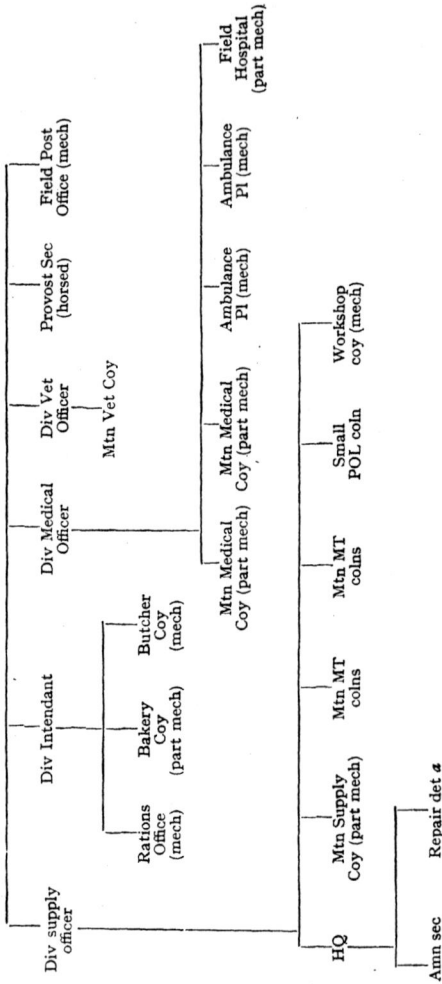

TABLE 32

Div supply officer

Div Intendant
- Rations Office (mech)
- Bakery Coy (part mech)
- Butcher Coy (mech)

Mtn Supply Coy (part mech)
- HQ
- Ann sec
- Repair det a

Div Medical Officer

Mtn Medical Coy (part mech)

Mtn Medical Coy (part mech)
- Ambulance Pl (mech)
- Ambulance Pl (mech)
- Field Hospital (part mech)

Div Vet Officer

Mtn Vet Coy

Provost Sec (horsed)

Field Post Office (mech)

Mtn MT colns

Mtn MT colns

Small POL coln

Workshop coy (mech)

Strength (estimated): 3,262 all ranks.
Fire-power: 30 LMGs.

NOTE.—(i) The armament of the services varies considerably. 30 LMGs is a typical allotment for services organized as above. A certain number of 2-cm (·79-in) AA A tk guns may also be included.

(ii) The strength given is an estimate only. It is based on the assumption that units under div sup off have a carrying capacity of 200 tons.

TABL

MOUNTAIN DIVISION

Divisional HQ

Service

Mtn Engineer Bn

Lt M
Eng Co
(mec

Bridging
Coln *b*

Reser
Equipm
& Sto
2 LM(

Lt Mech
Coy
(as in Armd Div)

Bridging
Coln *b* (mech)

HQ   1 Pl   2 Pl   3 Pl   Supplen
tary
equipm

Pontoon & trestle
equipment

A tk Bn

HQ

1 Coy   2 Coy   3 Coy

Each nine 5-cm (1·97-in) A tk guns
6 LMGs

Mtn Arty Regt

HQ

Mtn Eng
Coy

Mtn Eng
Coy

HQ & Sig Pl
2 LMGs

HQ & Sig Pl
2 LMGs

Pl   Pl   Pl

Sec   Sec   Sec

Sec

Each 3 LMGs

Mtn Rifle Regt

HQ

III Bn

16 A tk Coy
nine 5-cm (1·97-in)
A tk guns
6 LMGs

II Bn

I Bn

5 Hy Coy

4 MG Coy

12 MMGs,
six 8-cm
(3-in) mortars

(*a*) Pnr Pl 3 LMGs
(*b*) Mtn Gun Pl, 2
7·5-cm (2·95-in)
Mtn guns
(*c*) Hy Mortar Pl, 4
12-cm (4·71-in)
mortars
(*d*) A tk Pl, 4 2·8-cm
(1·1-in) A tk
guns, 2 LMGs

HQ Coy

Sig Pl   Mtd Inf Pl   Pnr Pl
3 LMGs

1 Rifle Coy   2 Rifle Coy   3 Rifle Coy

Each: 12 LMGs, three 5-cm (2-in) mortars,
3 A tk rifles

Mtn Rifle Regt

Mtn Rifle Regt

Sigs Bn

HQ

Telephone
Coy
10 LMGs

Wireless
Coy
6 LMGs

Lt Sig
Coln
1 LMG

Recce
(Cyclist)
Coy

Recce
(Cyclist)
Coy

Hy Coy

ch 9 LMGs three 5-cm
(2-in) mortars

ltn Gun Pl,   A tk Pl
wo 7·5-cm
(2·95-in)
Mtn guns

Med Mortar Pl
six 8-cm
(3-in) mortars

three 2·8-cm
(1·1-in)
A tk guns
3 LMGs

IV Bty

Tp   Tp   Tp

Each four 10·5-cm (4·14-in) Mtn hows,
2 LMGs

Lt Arty Coln

III Bty

HQ Tp   Survey
Sec

Sig Sec

II Bty

Lt Arty Coln

I Bty

Tp   Tp   Tp

Each four 7·5-cm (2·95-in) Lt Mtn guns,
2 LMGs

HQ & Sig Sec

HQ Tp   Survey Sec

Sig Sec

Note.—The organization given should be regarded as provisional, since complete information is lacking. The organization of mountain
divisions is very flexible, and the allocation of weapons will vary according to the type of country in which the division is operating.

MOUNTAIN DIVISION—SUMMARY OF PERSONNEL AND WEAPONS

Unit	Per-sonnel	Small Arms			AA/and/or A tk guns			Mortars			Close support and Divisional Artillery	
		LMGs	MMGs	A tk Rifles	2-cm (·79-in) AA/A tk gun	2·8-cm (1·1-in) A tk gun	5-cm (1·97-in) A tk gun	5-cm (2-in) Mortar	8-cm (3-in) Mortar	12-cm (4·71-in) Mortar	7·5-cm (2·95-in) Lt mtn gun	10·5-cm (4·14-in) Mtn how
HQ ...	152	—	—	—	—	—	—	—	—	—	—	—
Recce Unit ...	561	21	4	—	—	3	—	6	6	—	2	—
Sigs Bn ...	398	17	—	—	—	—	—	—	—	—	—	—
Two Mtn Rifle Regts... ...	7,000	264	72	54	—	24	18	54	36	24?	12	—
Mtn Arty Regt...	2,780	24	—	—	—	—	—	—	—	—	36	12
A tk Bn... ...	550	18 (16)	—	—	(12)	—	27 (18)	—	—	—	—	—
Eng Bn ...	1,043	29	—	—	—	—	—	—	—	—	—	—
Services... ...	3,262	30	—	—	—	—	—	—	—	—	—	—
Total... ...	15,746	403 (401)	76	54	(12)	27	45 (36)	60	42	24?	50	12

Note.—(i) *A tk bns*: Bns equipped with 7·5-cm (2·95-in) A tk guns in place of 5-cm (1·97-in) guns will be encountered. Figures in brackets are for a bn, of which the third coy is an AA coy.

(ii) *Transport*: As information concerning the transport of mountain units is incomplete no estimate of vehicle holdings and horses has been included. The allotment of pack, horse-drawn and motor transport will vary considerably according to the type of country in which the division is operating.

CHAPTER V

SECTION 27.—GHQ—TROOPS

NOTES.—(1) Only those GHQ combatant units are included in this "Pocket Book" of which the organization is known in some detail. Reference may be made to "The German Forces in the Field, Part D," and "New Notes on the German Army No. 3, Engineers" for other specialist units which are known to exist.

(2) Non-divisional supply and administrative units are discussed in outline in Part I, Chapter III, of this Pocket Book, and in detail in "New Notes on the German Army No. 4, Supply Services."

(a) *Organization* :

MOTORIZED MG BATTALION

TABLE 34

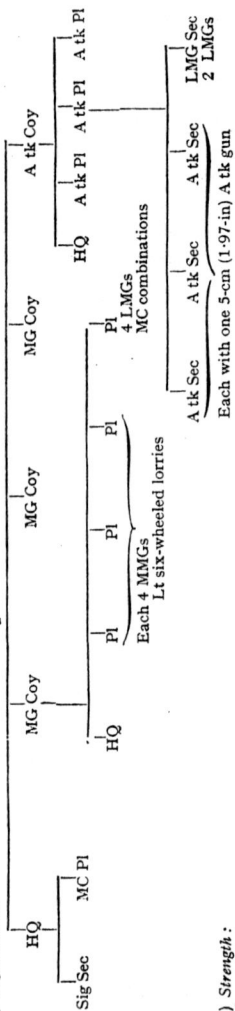

(b) *Strength* :

	Officers	Other ranks	Motorcycles, medium, solo	Motorcycles, heavy, with sidecars	Motor vehicles
MG Bn ...	25	955	80	76	173
HQ incl MC Pl	6	104	7	10	33
MG Coy ...	5	234	22	18	38
A tk Coy ...	4	149	7	12	26

(c) *Fire-power* :

	LMGs	MMGs	5-cm (1·97-in) A tk guns
Bn			
HQ incl MC Pl	22?	36	9
MG Coy ...	4	12	—
A tk Coy ...	6	—	9

TABLE 35

MOTORIZED AA BN

HQ
Sig Pl (with 6 pack WT secs)

Coy
Coy
Coy (not included in all bns)

Coy

HQ and Sig Pl
(4 pack WT secs
1 lt tele sec)

1 Pl
2 Pl
3 Pl
as 1 Pl

Half Pl
Half Pl

Each two 2-cm (·79-in) guns

or

1 Pl
2 Pl
(as 1 Pl)
3 Pl

Two four-barrelled
2-cm (·79-in) guns

Half Pl
Half Pl

Each two 2-cm (·79-in) guns

Fire-power and strength (approx) :

Four Coy Bn

Forty-eight 2-cm (·79-in) guns. *Strength* : 800 all ranks ; or
Thirty-two 2-cm (·79-in) guns } *Strength* : 800 all ranks
Eight 2-cm (·79-in) four barrelled guns }

Three Coy Bn

Thirty-six 2-cm (·79-in) guns. *Strength* : 600 all ranks ; or
Twenty-four 2-cm (·79-in) guns } *Strength* : 600 all ranks
Six 2-cm (·79-in) four barrelled guns }

NOTE.—Guns may be self-propelled or tractor-drawn.

TABLE 36

HEAVY INFANTRY GUN COY

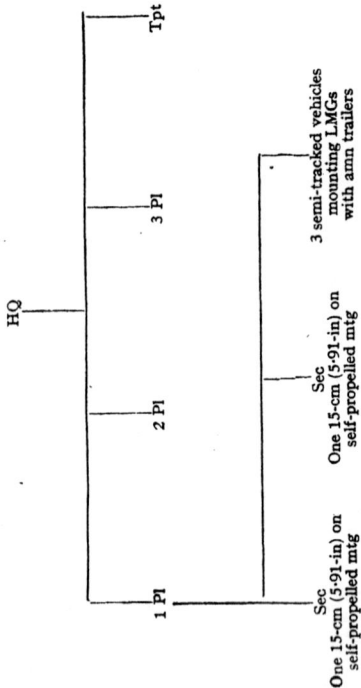

HQ

1 Pl   2 Pl   3 Pl   Tpt

Sec
One 15-cm (5·91-in) on
self-propelled mtg

Sec
One 15-cm (5·91-in) on
self-propelled mtg

3 semi-tracked vehicles
mounting LMGs
with amn trailers

Strength : 4 officers, 172 ORs.
Fire-power : 15-cm (5·91-in) by inf guns on SP mountings   6

TABLE 37

HEAVY TANK BATTALION (INDEPENDENT)

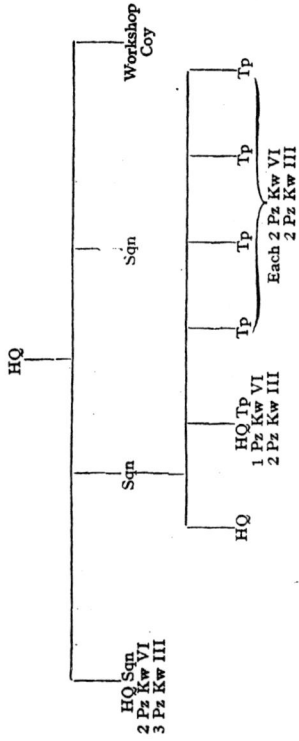

HQ

Sqn

Sqn

Workshop
Coy

HQ Sqn
2 Pz Kw VI
3 Pz Kw III

HQ
1 Pz Kw VI
2 Pz Kw III

HQ Tp

Tp   Tp   Tp   Tp

Each 2 Pz Kw VI
2 Pz Kw III

Strength (estimated) : 750 all ranks.

Tanks :
    20 Pz Kw VI
    23 Pz Kw III [a proportion of which mount the short 7·5-cm (2·95-in) tank gun).

NOTE.—This is the organization of a heavy tank battalion in Tunisia. The organization
    of a heavy tank battalion forming part of a tank regiment is not known.

FLAME-THROWING TANK BATTALION

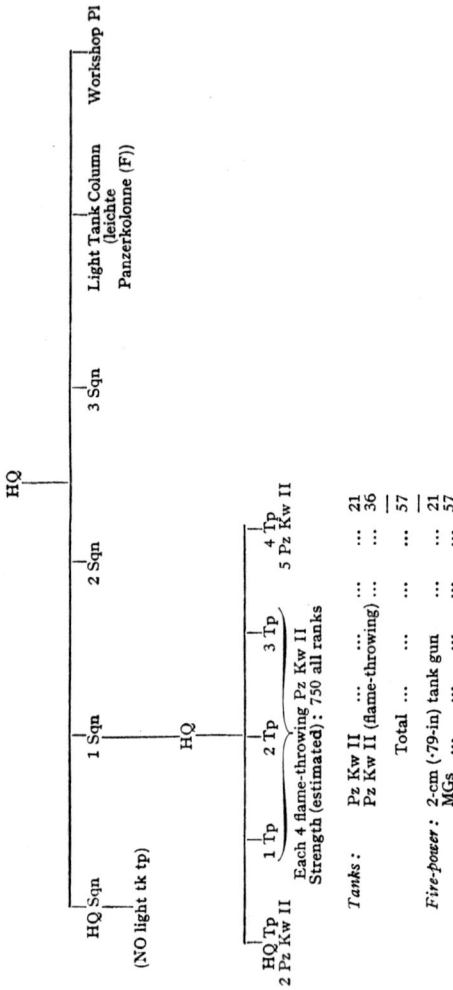

TABLE 38

HQ

| HQ Sqn | 1 Sqn | 2 Sqn | 3 Sqn | Light Tank Column (leichte Panzerkolonne (F)) | Workshop Pl |

(NO light tk tp)

HQ

HQ Tp
2 Pz Kw II   1 Tp   2 Tp   3 Tp   4 Tp
                                      5 Pz Kw II

Each 4 flame-throwing Pz Kw II
Strength (estimated) : 750 all ranks

Tanks :	Pz Kw II	...	...	...	...	21
	Pz Kw II (flame-throwing)	...	...	...	36
	Total	...	...	...	...	57
Fire-power :	2-cm (·79-in) tank gun	...	...	21
	MGs	...	...	...	...	57

NOTES.—(i) *Fuel supply for flame-throwers.*—One charging is carried in each flame-throwing tank; two further chargings in standard containers on two lorries per platoon in coy tpt ; a fourth charging in barrels in light tank column.

(ii) Figures for *fire-power* do not include any weapons there may be at bn HQ and HQ sqn.

(iii) The replacement of Pz Kw II (either as a flame-throwing tank or with normal armament) by Pz Kw III is to be expected, as Pz Kw III are released from normal tank regiments re-equipped with " Panthers."

TABLE 39

ASSAULT GUN BTY.

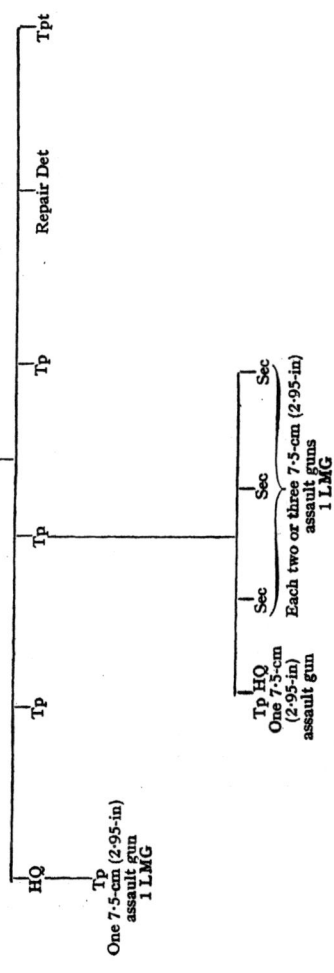

HQ

Tpt

Repair Det

Tp

Tp

Tp

Tp — One 7·5-cm (2·95-in) assault gun, 1 LMG

HQ

Tp HQ — One 7·5-cm (2·95-in) assault gun

Sec · Sec · Sec — Each two or three 7·5-cm (2·95-in) assault guns, 1 LMG

Strength: · (Lower establishment) 450 all ranks.

Fire-power: 7·5-cm (2·95-in) assault guns 22 or 31

LMGs 10

MT: Mot vehicles (lower establishment) 130

MCs 41

ARMY AA BATTERY (HEERESFLAK)

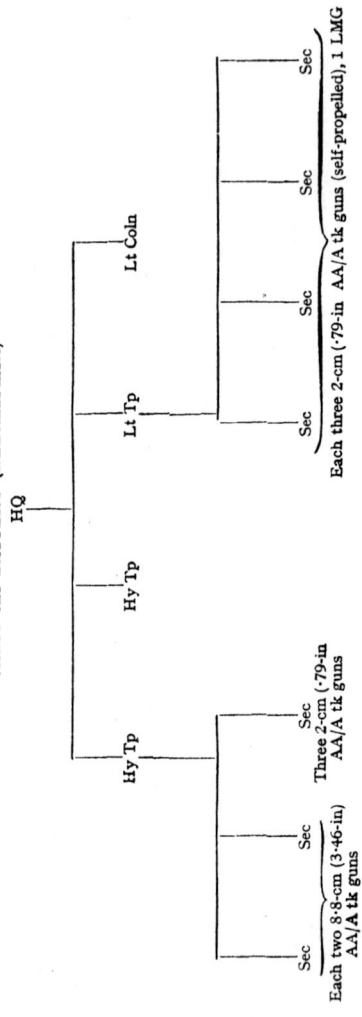

HQ

- Hy Tp
  - Sec — Each two 8·8-cm (3·46-in) AA/A tk guns
  - Sec — Three 2-cm (·79-in) AA/A tk guns
- Hy Tp
- Lt Tp
  - Sec
  - Sec
- Lt Coln
  - Sec
  - Sec

Each three 2-cm (·79-in AA/A tk guns (self-propelled), 1 LMG

Strength: 710 all ranks.

Fire-power:

LMGs	...	...	4
2-cm (·79-in) AA/A tk guns	...	...	18
8·8-cm (3·46-in) AA/A tk guns	...	...	8

TABLE 41

SMOKE REGIMENT

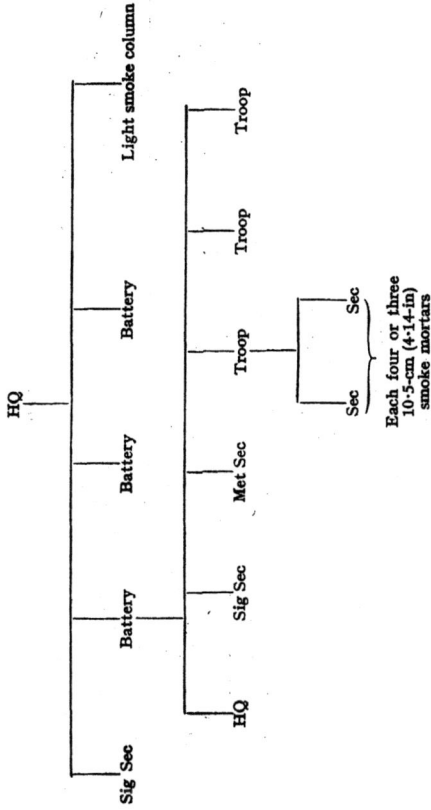

HQ

| Sig Sec | Battery | Battery | Battery | Light smoke column |

HQ | Sig Sec | Met Sec | Troop | Troop | Troop

Troop — { Sec ... Sec }

Each four or three
10·5-cm (4·14-in)
smoke mortars

Strength (lower est) : Approx. 1,800 all ranks.

Fire-power : 10·5-cm (4·14-cm) smoke mortars (higher est) ... 72
(lower est) ... 54

TABLE 42

SMOKE REGIMENT WITH 15-cm (5·91-in) SMOKE MORTARS 41

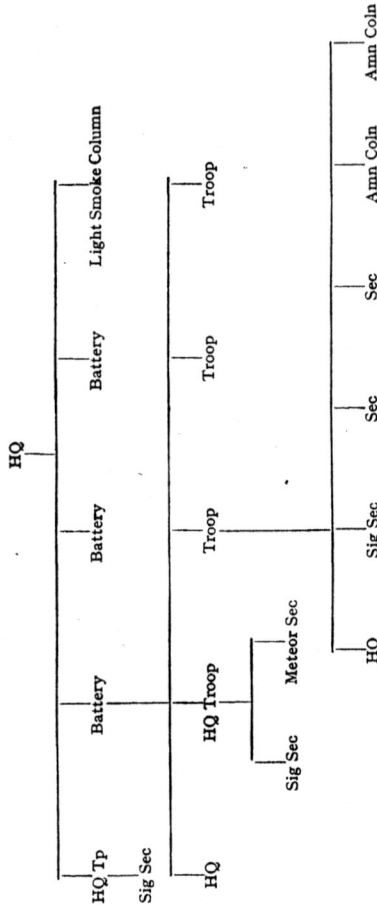

HQ

HQ Tp — Sig Sec

Battery | Battery | Battery | Battery | Light Smoke Column

HQ Troop — Sig Sec — Meteor Sec

HQ — Troop — Troop — Troop

HQ — Sig Sec — Sec — Sec — Troop

{ Each four or three 15-cm (5·91-in) mortars

Amn Coln | Amn Coln

Strength (lower establishment) 57 officers; 1,648 ORs.

Fire-power : 15-cm (5·91-in) smoke mortars (higher est) 72
                                (lower est) 54

MT : Mot vehicle (higher est) 417
                 (lower est) 378
     MCs 130

TABLE 43

SMOKE BATTERY WITH HEAVY PROJECTORS

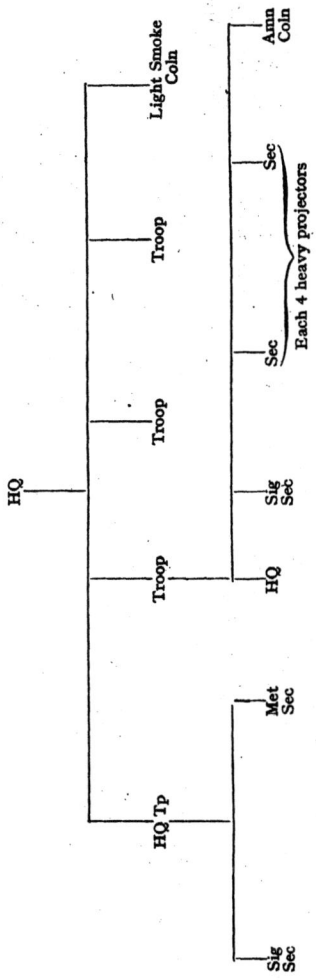

HQ

HQ Tp — Troop — Troop — HQ — Troop — Light Smoke Coln

Sig Sec

Met Sec

HQ — Sig Sec — Sec — Sec — Amn Coln

Each 4 heavy projectors

Strength : 19 officers, 560 ORs.

Fire-power : Heavy projectors 24

MT : Mot vehs 144

MCs 39

DECONTAMINATION (CONTAMINATION) BATTERY   TABLE 44

HQ

Sig Sec

HQ

Met Sec

Sig Sec

HQ

Tp — Sec — Sec
Each 3 gas scout vehs
6 med decontamination vehs

Tp

Tp

Light Decontamination Coln
3 Secs
9 vehs, each carrying 1·2 tons of decontaminant

Light Contamination Coln
3 Secs
36 med bulk contamination vehs
6 vehs with 100 portable sprayers

Strength: 22 officers, 718 ORs.

MT :
Gas scout vehs	...	...	...	...	18
Med decontamination vehs	...	...	...	...	36
Med bulk contamination vehs	...	...	...	36
Personal decontamination vehs	...	...	...	3
Clothing decontamination vehs	...	...	...	1
Mobile field laboratory	...	...	...	1
Other mot vehs (estimated)	...	...	...	110
Total ...	...	...	...	205	mot vehs
MCs ...	...	...	...	49	

NOTES.— (i) The battery carries the following stores:—
Protective clothing sets	...	...	...	1,200
Decontamination drums	...	...	...	576
Gas containers ...	...	...	...	600
Persistent toxic substances	...	...	...	42 tons

(ii) When the battery is to undertake contamination, the medium bulk contamination vehs and portable sprayers are issued to troops from the light contamination column, the medium decontamination vehicles being withdrawn from troops to the light decontamination column.

TABLE 45

ROAD DECONTAMINATION BATTERY

HQ

Sig Sec

HQ Tp
2 gas scout vehs

Tp
HQ
2 gas scout vehs

Tp
Decontamination Sec
3 lt decontamination vehs
6 med decontamination vehs

Tp

Equipment and Stores Sec
5 med lorries

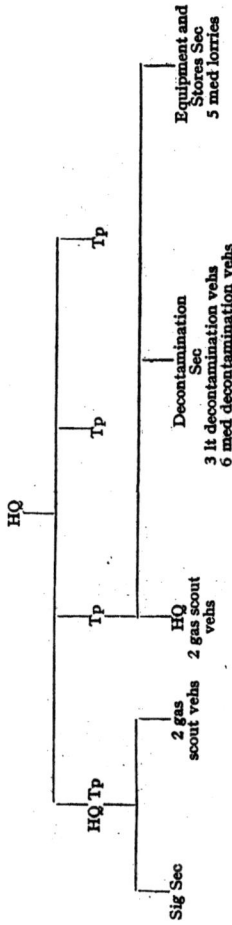

Strength : 7 officers, 224 ORs.

MT :
Gas scout vehs...	...	8
Lt decontamination vehs	...	9
Med decontamination vehs	...	18
Other motor vehs	...	41
Total	...	76 mot vehs
MCs	...	12

NOTE.—The battery carries 42·5 tons of decontaminant.

RAILWAY ENGINEER REGIMENT

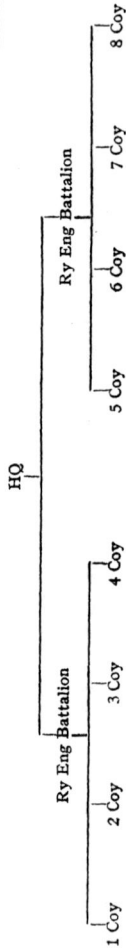

TABLE 46

HQ

Ry Eng Battalion — 1 Coy · 2 Coy · 3 Coy · 4 Coy

Ry Eng Battalion — 5 Coy · 6 Coy · 7 Coy · 8 Coy

BRIDGE-BUILDING BATTALION

TABLE 47

HQ

Bridge-building Coy · Bridge-building Coy · Bridge-building Coy (Half-platoon)

Engineer Tools Platoon (Half-platoon)

Engineer Park Coy — Workshop Section

Strength:

Bridge-building Coy ...	...	210 all ranks (estimate)
Engineer Tools Platoon ...	...	116 ,, ,, ,,
Engineer Park Coy ...	...	192 ,, ,, ,,
Total in battalion ...	...	1,148
With HQ, total ...	...	1,209

NOTE.—*Railway bridge building battalions* appear to be organized in the same way as bridge-building battalions, containing four companies, a railway engineer tools platoon and a railway engineer park company.

TABLE 48

ASSAULT BOAT COMPANY

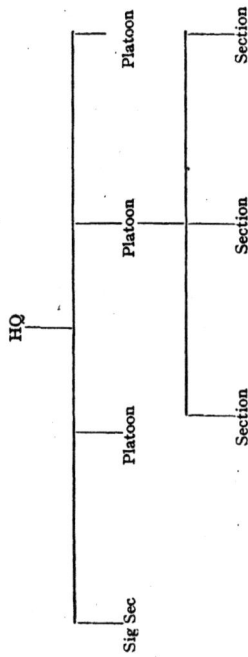

HQ

Sig Sec | Platoon | Platoon | Platoon

Section | Section | Section

Strength: All ranks 194

Fire-power: LMGs 4
A tk rifles 3

Equipment: Assault boats 36

NOTE.—Recent practice appears to be to make up assault boat detachments (*Kommando*) of varying size for service where required. The most usual type has three platoons with 81 assault boats in all.

ASSAULT ENGINEER COMPANY

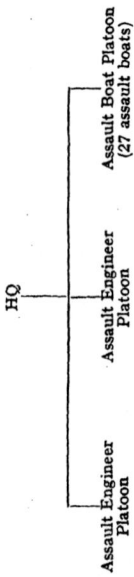

TABLE 49

HQ
- Assault Engineer Platoon
- Assault Engineer Platoon
- Assault Boat Platoon (27 assault boats)

Total personnel about 200.

CONSTRUCTION BATTALION

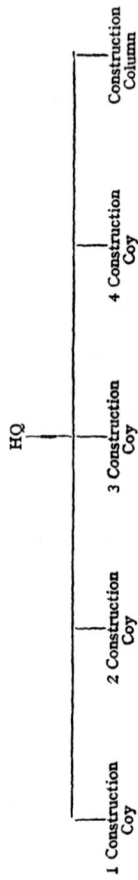

TABLE 50

HQ
- 1 Construction Coy
- 2 Construction Coy
- 3 Construction Coy
- 4 Construction Coy
- Construction Column

Strength: Approx. 1,900 all ranks.

NOTE.—Some battalions include one or more concrete construction companies (*Betonbaukompanien*).

TABLE 51

ROAD CONSTRUCTION BATTALIONS

1. ROAD CONSTRUCTION BATTALION

Strength: 1,500 (approx)

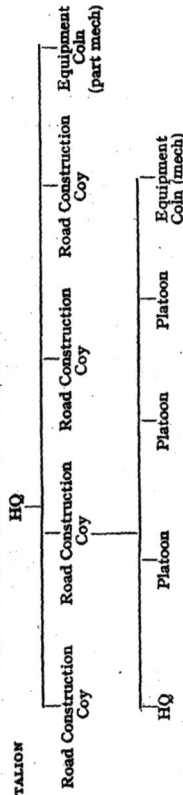

HQ

- HQ
- Road Construction Coy
- Road Construction Coy
- Road Construction Coy
- Road Construction Coy
- Road Construction Coy
- Equipment Coln (part mech)

Platoon — Platoon — Platoon — Platoon — Equipment Coln (mech)

2. LIGHT ROAD CONSTRUCTION BATTALION

Strength: 750 (approx)

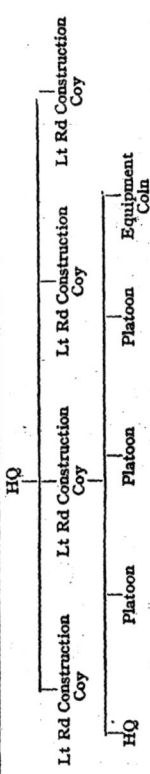

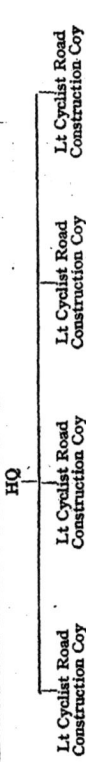

HQ

- HQ
- Lt Rd Construction Coy
- Lt Rd Construction Coy
- Lt Rd Construction Coy
- Lt Rd Construction Coy
- Lt Rd Construction Coy

Platoon — Platoon — Platoon — Platoon — Equipment Coln

3. LIGHT CYCLIST ROAD CONSTRUCTION BATTALION

Strength: 750 (approx)

HQ

- Lt Cyclist Road Construction Coy
- Lt Cyclist Road Construction Coy
- Lt Cyclist Road Construction Coy
- Lt Cyclist Road Construction Coy
- Lt Cyclist Road Construction Coy

GHQ SIGNALS REGIMENT (MECH)

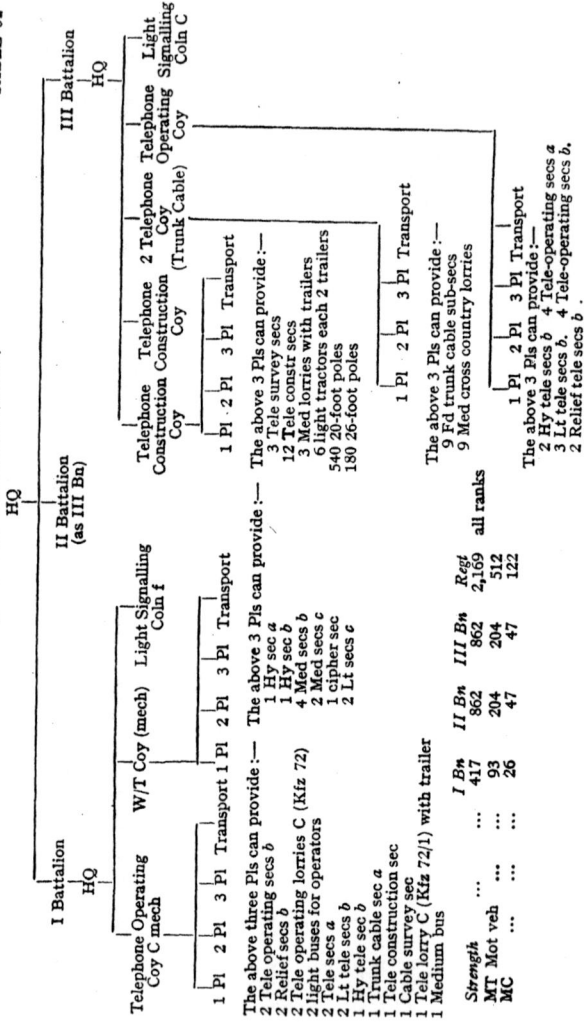

TABLE 52

HQ

I Battalion
HQ

II Battalion
(as III Bn)
HQ

III Battalion
HQ

I Battalion

Telephone Operating
Coy C mech

W/T Coy (mech)

Light Signalling
Coln f

1 Pl 2 Pl 3 Pl Transport

1 Pl 2 Pl 3 Pl Transport

The above three Pls can provide:—
2 Tele operating secs *b*
2 Relief secs *b*
2 Tele operating lorries C (Kfz 72)
2 light buses for operators
2 Tele secs *a*
2 Lt tele secs *b*
1 Hy tele sec *b*
1 Trunk cable sec *a*
1 Tele construction sec
1 Cable survey sec
1 Tele lorry C (Kfz 72/1) with trailer
1 Medium bus

The above 3 Pls can provide:—
1 Hy sec *a*
1 Hy sec *b*
4 Med secs *b*
2 Med secs *c*
1 cipher sec
2 Lt secs *c*

III Battalion

Light
Signalling
Coln C

Telephone
Construction
Coy

Telephone
Construction
Coy

2 Telephone
Coy
(Trunk Cable)

Telephone
Operating
Coy

1 Pl 2 Pl 3 Pl Transport

The above 3 Pls can provide:—
3 Tele survey secs
12 Tele constr secs
3 Med lorries with trailers
6 light tractors each 2 trailers
540 20-foot poles
180 26-foot poles

1 Pl 2 Pl 3 Pl Transport

The above 3 Pls can provide:—
9 Fd trunk cable sub-secs
9 Med cross country lorries

1 Pl 2 Pl 3 Pl Transport

The above 3 Pls can provide:—
2 Hy tele secs *b*   4 Tele-operating secs *a*
3 Lt tele secs *b*.   4 Tele-operating secs *b*.
2 Relief tele secs *b* .

Strength		I Bn	II Bn	III Bn	Regt
MT	...	417	862	862	2,169
Mot veh	...	93	204	204	512
MC	...	26	47	47	122

all ranks

TABLE 53

TELEPHONE TRUNK CABLE COMPANY (*Fsp FFK Kp.*)

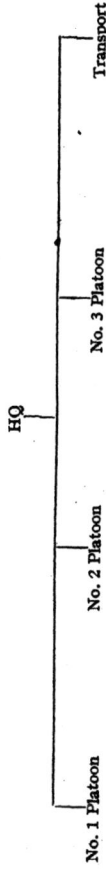

```
                        HQ
        ┌────────────┬──┴──────────┬──────────────┐
   No. 1 Platoon  No. 2 Platoon  No. 3 Platoon  Transport
```

The above three platoons produce :—
9 telephone trunk cable sections *c*.
3 line repair sections (mech).
MT : 19

TELEPHONE CONSTRUCTION COMPANY

TABLE 54

```
                    HQ
    ┌──────────┬──────────┬──────────┐
1 Platoon   2 Platoon   3 Platoon   Transport
```

The above three platoons can produce:—
    3 telephone survey sections
    12 telephone construction sections
    3 medium lorries with trailers
    6 light tractors each with 2 trailers
    540 20-foot poles
    180 26-foot poles

Strength : 4 officers, 224 ORs
MT :   Mot vehs   ...   49
        Trailers   ...   21
        MCs   11

TELEPHONE OPERATING COY (*Fsp Bau Kp*)

TABLE 55

```
                    HQ
    ┌──────────┬──────────┬──────────┐
1 Platoon   2 Platoon   3 Platoon   Transport
```

The above three platoons can produce:—
    2 heavy telephone secs *b*.
    3 light telephone secs *b*.
    2 relief telephone secs *b*.
    4 telephone operating secs *a*.
    4 telephone operating secs *b*.

Strength : 4 officers, 142 ORs
MT :   Mot vehs   ...   37
        MCs   11

PART III

GERMAN AIR FORCE UNITS—
ORGANIZATION

CHAPTER I

AA ARTILLERY AND GAF FIELD
DIVISIONS

SECTION 28.—GENERAL

1. In addition to the normal bomber, fighter, and reconnaissance units of the GAF (the organization of which is beyond the scope of this Pocket Book), the following types of GAF units will be found operating with the army :—

(a) Anti-aircraft artillery (Flak) ⎫ dealt with in this
(b) GAF field divisions   ⎬   chapter

(c) Air-borne troops, dealt with in Chapter 2.

SECTION 29.—ANTI-AIRCRAFT ARTILLERY
(FLAK)

1. Under the German system, AA defence both in the home country and in the theatres of war is in the main the responsibility of the German air force, though the German army also has certain AA units of its own (see page 15). In theatres of war GAF AA units employed in static defence, mainly in rear areas, remain entirely under the control of the GAF, and are therefore not further considered in this Pocket Book. In any given theatre, however, a considerable portion of the GAF AA units will during active operations come under the operational control of the army, though they will continue to be supplied and administered by the GAF.

2. GAF AA units in the field are organized in batteries, regiments, divisions, and corps. The basic unit is the battery. There is no fixed establishment for the regiment, division, or corps. These are essentially staffs, controlling a number of batteries, regiments, or divisions (as the case may be), the number depending on tactical requirements.

3. Just as in the GAF there is no fixed establishment for any unit above the battery, so in the army there is no fixed establishment for higher formations. The number of divisions in a corps, and corps in an army is not fixed, and frequently changes during active operations. It follows therefore that it is impossible to lay down any standard allotment of GAF AA units to army formations. Usually, however, the GAF AA corps operates at army group level, the GAF AA division at army, and the GAF AA regiment at corps level. The following hypothetical example is given to illustrate the probable order of allotment of GAF AA units to army formations. A corps in the German army might consist of one armoured, two motorized, and two infantry divisions. During active operations the probable allotment to a corps would be a GAF AA regiment. This regiment might consist of three " mixed " and one light battery (for organization *see* page 99). The corps commander would allot the AA batteries to his divisions in accordance with the tactical requirements of the situation, and the advice of the GAF AA regiment commander.

4. In addition to their AA role, GAF AA units allotted to the army are employed as a highly mobile and powerful striking force against ground targets and in particular as a valuable reinforcement of the army's anti-tank fire-power, since all German AA guns employed in the field are also designed for use in the anti-tank role. GAF AA units may be employed in conjunction with spearheads, composed of armoured and motorized forces, or with non-motorized forces, for forcing river crossings, penetrating fortified lines, and providing defence against enemy tanks. They may also be deployed as highly mobile artillery in support of tank attacks or thrown in at points where enemy pressure is very great.

Section 30.—GAF FIELD DIVISIONS

1. As a result of man-power difficulties in Germany it was decided in the autumn of 1942 to " comb out " surplus personnel from the GAF ground staffs, AA units, and GAF Initial Training Wings (Fliegerregimenter), and to form them into some twenty GAF field divisions with the necessary depot and training units.

2. The GAF field division resembles the motorized division of the army in its artillery component, which consists of two field, one medium, and one AA batteries. In other respects, however, the GAF field division resembles the light division of the army.
It includes two rifle (Jaeger) regiments, each of three

GAF MIXED AA BATTERY (MECH)

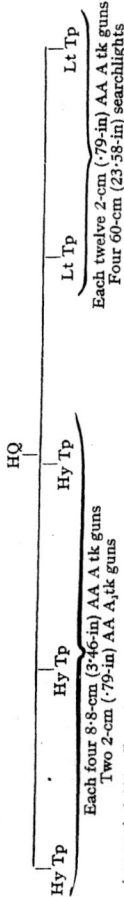

TABLE 56

```
                              HQ
                              |
     Hy Tp      Hy Tp      Hy Tp        Lt Tp      Lt Tp
```

Each four 8·8-cm (3·46-in) AA A tk guns
Two 2-cm (·79-in) AA A,tk guns

Each twelve 2-cm (·79-in) AA A tk guns
Four 60-cm (23·58-in) searchlights

Strength: (approx) 1,300 all ranks.
Fire-power: 8·8-cm (3·46-in) guns 12
2-cm (·79-in) guns... 30

Notes.— (i) Heavy troops, equipped with six 8·8-cm (3·46-in) and three 2-cm (·79-in) AA A tk guns will also be encountered.
(ii) Units in the field, especially in forward areas, frequently dispense with their searchlights.

GAF LIGHT AA BATTERY (MECH)

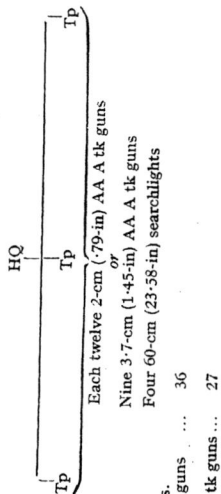

TABLE 57

```
                 HQ
                 |
       Tp        Tp        Tp
```

Each twelve 2-cm (·79-in) AA A tk guns
or
Nine 3·7-cm (1·45-in) AA A tk guns
Four 60-cm (23·58-in) searchlights

Strength: (approx) 950 all ranks.
Fire-power: 2-cm (·79-in) AA A tk guns ... 36
or
3·7-cm (1·45-in) AA A tk guns ... 27

Note.—Units in the field, especially in forward areas, frequently dispense with their searchlights

GAF FIELD DIVISION

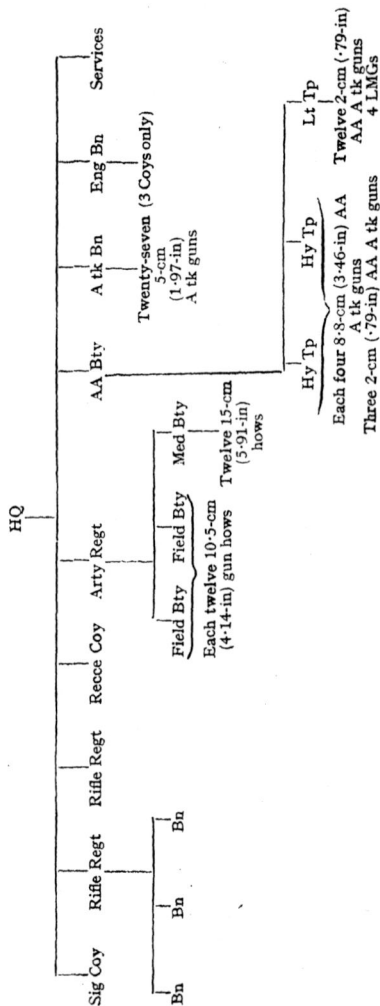

HQ

Sig Coy | Rifle Regt | Rifle Regt | Recce Coy | Arty Regt | AA Bty | A tk Bn | Eng Bn | Services

Rifle Regt: Bn — Bn — Bn

Arty Regt — Field Bty, Field Bty, Med Bty
Each twelve 10·5-cm (4·14-in) gun hows
Twelve 15-cm (5·91-in) hows

A tk Bn — Twenty-seven (3 Coys only) 5-cm (1·97-in) A tk guns

AA Bty — Hy Tp, Hy Tp, Lt Tp
Each four 8·8-cm (3·46-in) AA A tk guns
Three 2-cm (·79-in) AA A tk guns
Twelve 2-cm (·79-in) AA A tk guns
4 LMGs

Eng Bn — (3 Coys only)

NOTE.—The above is believed to be the intended establishment of a GAF field division. Some divisions fall considerably below this standard in organization and equipment.

Strength: (approx) 10,000 all ranks.

Fire-power :

5-cm (2-in) mortars ...	57
8-cm (3-in) mortars ...	36
2-cm (·79-in) AA A tk guns ...	18
5-cm (1·97-in) A tk guns ...	27
8·8-cm (3·46-in) AA A tk guns ...	8
10·5-cm (4·14-in) gun hows ...	24
15-cm (5·91-in) hows ...	12

battalions, and the divisional units (other than the artillery) are on a reduced scale. It appears probable that some GAF field divisions, like the light divisions, may rely on transport from the GHQ pool to pick up the personnel in the rifle regiments, while other GAF field divisions are definitely organized on a horse-drawn basis.

3. The organizational table at page 100 gives the intended establishment of the GAF field divisions. Some GAF field divisions fall considerably below this standard, since much hasty improvisation was necessary in their formation. Though some divisions have been used in first line fighting, others, employed on airfield defence, L of C duties, coast defence, etc., cannot be regarded as the equivalents of army divisions.

CHAPTER 2

AIRBORNE TROOPS AND GAF TRANSPORT

SECTION 31.—AIRBORNE TROOPS— ORGANIZATION

1. German airborne troops may be divided into :—

(a) GAF airborne troops (mainly parachute troops).

(b) Air landing troops, who are army personnel.

2. Army air landing troops may in practice be provided by any army formation or unit, which has been trained in emplaning and deplaning. 22 Infantry Division was however employed in an air landing role in Holland in 1940, and it is organized on a series of war establishments specially adapted for air landing operations. No details of these war establishments are available, but it is probable that the actual organization of 22 Infantry Division in air-landing operations would be specially adapted to meet the immediate tactical requirements.

3. GAF airborne troops are organized in Air Corps (*Fliegerkorps*) XI, which also includes a number of glider towing units, and assumes operational control of air transport aircraft required for an airborne operation.

4. Airborne troops in Air Corps XI include the following :—

Corps troops—

Demonstration battalion.

MG battalion.

Corps parachute engineer battalion.

AA battalion (*Fallsch Fla Abt*).

Signals battalion (*Luftnachrichten Abt* 41).

Propaganda platoon.

Medical unit.

Field hospital (air landing).

Parachute divisions (Fallschirmjaeger division). Probably two, each intended to have the following establishment :—

Three parachute rifle regiments.

· Parachute artillery regiment.

Parachute A tk battalion.

Parachute engineer battalion.

Signals unit, and signals operating company.·

The organization of these units, in so far as it is known, is set out in pages 103-106.

5. Though it would probably still be possible for the Germans, should the strategic need again arise, to mount a large scale airborne attack comparable with that on Crete (where the whole of 7 Parachute Division and a substantial allotment of corps troops were employed), they would undoubtedly now have difficulty in finding the requisite number of transport aircraft for such an operation and in achieving air superiority over so large an area. It is therefore more probable that the Germans will continue their present policy of employing parachute troops in smaller groups, which, available as they are to be rushed to seriously threatened theatres, have proved their value in Libya and Tunisia. These groups have been employed primarily in ground fighting alongside units of the German army, but would also have been available at short notice, had the tactical need arisen and the transport aircraft been available, to revert to their proper airborne role.

6. The Parachute Brigade Ramcke, which was sent to North Africa at the beginning of August, 1942, may be taken as a typical example of such a group. It consisted of :—

Three parachute rifle battalions.

Five companies of the demonstration battalion of Air Corps XI with a troop of heavy projectors under command.

A battery, including four troops of parachute artillery equipped with 7·5-cm (2·95-in) and 10·5-cm (4·14-in) light recoilless guns.

At least one anti-tank company.

One engineer company.

Medical detachment.

Supply company with motor-cycle tractors.

7. The weakness of such a formation in artillery and other support weapons is apparent, a weakness which the parachutists' hard battle training, physical fitness, and *esprit de corps* have offset only at the cost of very heavy casualties.

TABLE 59

AIR CORPS XI

HQ

First level under HQ:
- Demonstration Bn
- Para Eng Bn (see Table 60)
- Para MG Bn (3 coys)
- Para AA Bn (4 coys)
- Para Division
- Propaganda Pl
- Medical Unit (4 coys)
- Field Hospital
- Tpt Echelon (Staffel)
- Supply Bn
- Bakery Coy
- Workshop Coy
- MT Workshop Pl

Under Para Division:
- Sig Bn
- Para Rifle Regt (see Table 61)
- Para Rifle Regt
- Para Rifle Regt
- Para Arty Regt
- Para Eng Bn
- Para A tk Bn
- Services

Under Para Arty Regt:
- HQ
- Bty (see Table 62)
- Bty

Under Services:
- Tpt Coy
- Tpt Echelon (Staffel)

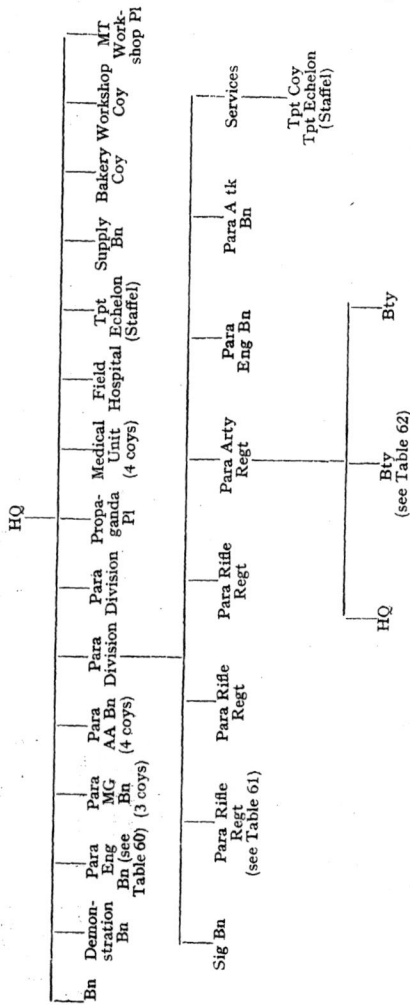

NOTES.—(i) The above table should be regarded as provisional, since information about changes in organization since the attack on Crete is incomplete.

(ii) The corps sig bn, supply bn, bakery coy, tpt echelon, workshop coy, MT workshop pl, and transport echelon are not air-borne. The field hospital is airlanding only.

TABLE 60

CORPS PARACHUTE ENGINEER BATTALION

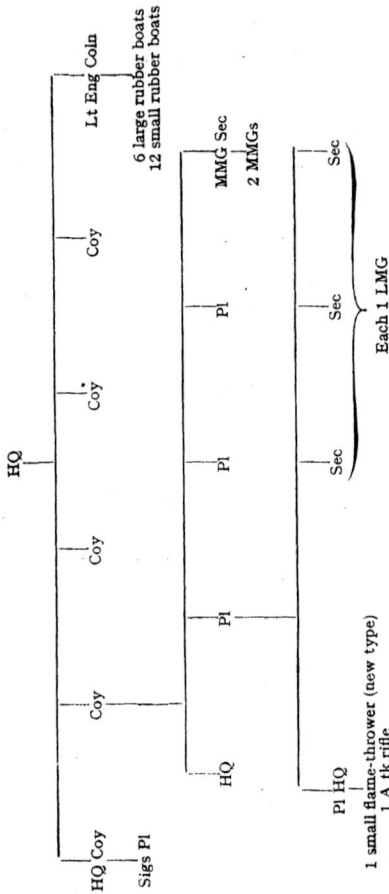

HQ

HQ Coy — Coy — Coy — Coy — Coy — Coy — Lt Eng Coln

Sigs Pl

6 large rubber boats
12 small rubber boats

HQ — Pl — Pl — Pl — MMG Sec

2 MMGs

Pl HQ — Sec — Sec — Sec — Sec

Each 1 LMG

1 small flame-thrower (new type)
1 A tk rifle

Strength (approx.) : 716 all ranks.

Fire-power :

LMGs	... ...	36
MMGs	... ...	8
A tk rifles ...	... ...	12
Small flame-thrower (new type)	... ...	12

NOTES.— (i) Organization, strength and fire-power should be regarded as provisional, since information is incomplete.

(ii) It is not known whether there is any standard allotment of engineer stores to the battalion. Personnel are intensively trained in the use of mines and demolition stores of all types (including those used in assaults on fixed defences). Stores actually carried on an operation will be carefully selected in accordance with tactical requirements.

PARACHUTE RIFLE REGT

TABLE 61

HQ

I Bn — II Bn — III Bn — 13 Inf Gun Coy 7·5-cm (2·95-in) mtn guns or light recoilless guns — 14 A tk Coy 2·8-cm (1·1-in) A tk guns or 4·2-cm (1·65-in) A tk guns

HQ Coy
Sig Pl — Pnr Pl

HQ — Sig Pl — Pnr Pl — 1 Rifle Coy — 2 Rifle Coy — 3 Rifle Coy — 4 Hy Coy

9 Rifle Coy — 10 Rifle Coy — 11 Rifle Coy — 12 Hy Coy

5 Rifle Coy — 6 Rifle Coy — 7 Rifle Coy — 8 Hy Coy

HQ — Sig Pl — Rifle Pl — Rifle Pl — Rifle Pl — A tk Sec Two 2·8-cm (1·1-in) A tk guns — Lt Mortar Sec One 5-cm (2-in) mortar

HQ — LMG Sec — LMG Sec — LMG Sec
Each 2 LMGs

HQ — MMG Pl — MMG Pl — Rifle Pl (as in rifle Coy) — Med Mortar Sec Two 8-cm (3-in) mortars — A tk Sec Two 2·8-cm (1·1-in) A tk guns

Sec (2 MMGs) — Sec (2 MMGs)

Establishment strength: Approx. 3,100 all ranks.
Battle strength: Approx. 2,200 all ranks.
Fire-power:

LMGs	... ...	198	
MMGs	... ...	24	
5-cm (2-in) mortars	... ...	30	
8-cm (3-in) mortars	... ...	6	
7·5-cm (2·95-in) mtn (or lt recoilless) guns	...	8	
2·8-cm (1·1-in) A tk guns	...	33	
or			
2·8-cm (1·1-in) A tk guns	... ...	24	and
4·2-cm (1·65-in) A tk guns	... ...	9	

NOTE.—Considerable variations in organization to suit the tactical requirements of the operation in which the parachute rifle regiment is engaged must be expected.

The following variations have for example been noted in a parachute rifle regiment employed in ground fighting:—

(a) A tk secs in rifle companies were equipped with A tk rifles in place of 2·8-cm (1·1 in) A tk guns. The 14 A tk Coy was apparently to be equipped with nine 5-cm (1·97 in) A tk guns.

(b) The 13 Inf Gun Coy was equipped with nine 10·5-cm (4·14 in) light recoilless guns, seven (15-cm) (5·91 in) rocket projectors, and 3 A tk rifles.

PARACHUTE ARTILLERY BATTERY

TABLE 62

HQ

HQ — Tp — Tp — Tp

Sig Sec
6 W/T sub-secs (?)
1 Sig exchange (?)
det

Sig Sec

HQ

4 W/T
sub-secs

2 telephone
sub-secs

Gun Echelon

Gun Sec — Gun Sec

Each two 10·5-cm (4·14-in)
lt recoilless guns

Inf Pl

Sec Sec Sec Sec Sec Sec

Each 1 LMG

Battle Strength: 461 all ranks.
Fire-power:

10·5-cm (4·14-in) lt recoilless guns	...	...	12
LMGs ...	...	...	...	18
A tk rifles	...	...	...	6

Transport (air-borne):

MCs ...	...	...	...	4
MC combinations	...	...	18
Bicycles	...	...	...	6
Amn carts	...	...	...	24

Section 32.—AIRBORNE TROOPS—TACTICS

1. The objective of airborne troops (in their primary airborne role) is normally ground suitable for air landings or vital to enemy communications. Hence they have a high scale of such offensive armament as is light and easily portable, and are thoroughly rehearsed in independent aggressive methods. The normal procedure is to cover the area selected (which may be several miles in diameter) with bombing and dive-bombing, followed by the dropping of a wave of parachutists in some strength (accompanied possibly by gliderborne troops) to neutralize the AA and other defences and to dislocate communications. Several hours later, according to the development of the situation, strong parachute and gliderborne reinforcements will be dropped, but only where the first wave has been successful.

2. Airborne troops normally work by formed units. They are highly trained in street and house fighting. They are not saboteurs (who are specially trained troops who will be dropped separately in small bodies, generally of from 6-10 men). Parachute troops are normally part of the major tactical plan.

Section 33.—GAF AIR TRANSPORT ORGANIZATION

1. The basic air transport organization is the wing (*Gruppe*) composed of four squadrons (*Staffeln*) each of 12 Ju 52 aircraft, and a wing HQ (*Gruppenstab*) of 5 aircraft, though wings equipped with obsolescent Heinkel 111 bombers are also known. The primary function of these wings is the transport of supplies for the army and air force, and they are usually under control of air fleets (*Luftflotten*).

2. When large numbers of transport formations are required as, for example, when the Sixth Army was encircled at STALINGRAD and had to be supplied by air, additional air transport wings may be formed by withdrawing Ju 52 or other aircraft from the air training schools.

3. Air transport wings may be formed, when required for a large scale operation into transport groups " for special employment " (*Kampfgeschwader zbV*). These groups are of varying size and are usually disbanded as soon as the purpose for which they were formed has been accomplished, though one group—*KG, zbV* 1—has survived throughout the war, with an establishment of four wings and a total of 220 aircraft.

4. When an airborne operation is contemplated the necessary air transport formations are placed at the disposal of the GOC Air Transport of Air Corps XI (*Fliegerführer XI Fl Korps*). He is responsible to AOC Air Corps XI for emplaning the airborne troops and for setting them down on

enemy territory, whether by parachute, in towed gliders, or in aircraft landing on captured airfields.

5. Glider-towing units may be subordinated to air fleets (*Luftflotten*) but Air Corps XI is also known to have glider towing units of its own, under its GOC Air Transport. These include a number of glider towing wings organized into one or more groups (*Luftlandegeschwader*). Each wing is subdivided into four squadrons (*Staffeln*) of 15 towing aircraft with gliders. It is possible that two of the squadrons in each wing will be equipped with DFS 230 gliders and the other two with GO 242 gliders. The towing aircraft may be He 111 or Ju 52 for the GO 242s, and Do 17 or HS 126 or Avias for the DFS 230s. Air Corps XI also controls a limited number of the very large Me 321 gliders, which are towed by the twin-fuselage Heinkel with five engines.

6. The DFS 230 is the only glider which has so far been used for carrying troops into battle. It was so used in Belgium and in Crete. During the evacuation of the Kuban, however, both DFS 230s and GO 242s were employed on a large scale for carrying troops. It is obvious that parachute troops cannot jump from gliders, but there is a strong possibility that this form of transport might be used for conveying parachute troops to an area where they were suddenly needed. The gliders would in such circumstances aim at landing on an airfield or other suitable ground in friendly territory. There has recently been a notable tendency to concentrate gliders in areas where parachute troops are stationed, and both gliders and parachute troops are associated in their subordination to Air Corps XI.

7. Apart from the glider towing units subordinated to Air Corps XI, there exist so-called " Liaison detachments S " (*S = Schlepp*) subordinated to the ordinary GAF air transport organization. These are wings each consisting of one squadron of 15 DFS 230s and two squadrons of GO 242s and are exclusively used in freight-transport for the GAF or the army. Dive bomber wings are also equipped with DFS 230 gliders, in which they can transfer their equipment and ground personnel when moving to a new base.

8. The shortage of suitable tugs has induced the Germans to equip the GO 242 and Me 321 gliders with aero-engines, the powered versions being named GO 244 and Me 323 (*see* Table 76). Little has been heard of the GO 244, but the Me 323 has proved extremely valuable for transporting MT, guns, and other bulky freight, in areas where it is not unduly exposed to attack in the air. Me 323s are organized in wings of 25 each. They have been used for carrying troops, but there appears to be some prejudice against exploiting their full capacity of over 100 men, 70 being the highest figure yet met with.

PART IV

CONVENTIONAL SIGNS

SECTION 34.—GENERAL

1. The German system of conventional signs consists of a number of basic signs and supplementary signs, which are combined to represent various formations, units, and equipments. These signs are used not only for marking maps, but also in charts, showing the order of battle and organization of formations. Signs will also be seen on vehicles and equipment, with or without the divisional emblem (with which the conventional sign should not be confused) and on direction and location sign posts.

2. At the start of the present war, the Germans had an elaborate system of conventional signs, which is set out at length in Appendix XLVIII of "Notes on the German Army—War". This system has apparently been found too elaborate for use in the field, and two lists of amendments, one dated November, 1942, and the other January, 1943, have been issued with the object of simplifying the basic and supplementary signs for weapons and equipment.

3. The revised system of conventional signs is explained below. Intelligence officers must not however expect every captured organizational chart, map, or other document, to conform rigidly to this system, since allowances must always be made for the idiosyncracies of individual draftsmen, particularly in sometimes preferring the old signs to the new. Once the system is understood, however, it is generally possible to deduce the meaning of new or unknown signs.

SECTION 35.—BASIC SIGNS FOR HEADQUARTERS

The following basic signs are used for HQ :—

| Army GHQ | Army Gp | Army | Corps | Div | Bde | Regt | Bn Bty | Coy Sqn Tp |

Section 36.—BASIC SIGNS FOR BRANCHES OF THE SERVICE

The following are the basic signs for branches of the service :—

Inf	Mtn	MC	Tk	Other armd	A tk	Cav and Recce	Cyclist

Arty	AA Arty	Smoke	Svy	Engr	Ry Engr	Fortress Engr	Construc-tional units

HT Units	Sig	Sup Services	Med Services	Vet Services	TC Services	MP	Fd Postal Services

Section 37.—FORMATION AND UNIT HQ

Formation and unit HQ are indicated by a combination of the HQ sign with the sign for the appropriate branch of the service.

Examples

Pz Div HQ	Arty Regt in armd div	Armd Engr Bn

Section 38.—COMPANIES AND EQUIVALENT UNITS

Companies and equivalent units are indicated in various ways (and German practice is not entirely consistent).

    (a) *Basic sign of the branch of the service with thickened side.*

Examples :—

Inf coy   Tk sqn   A tk coy   Cav sqn   Sig coy

    (b) *Square with thickened side and basic sign for the branch of the service.*

Examples :—

Mtn rifle coy   Engr coy   Sup coy

    (c) *Weapon or equipment sign with thickened line.*

Examples :—

A tk coy   Armd car sqn

    (d) *Artillery troops.*

        Artillery troops are indicated by the weapon sign with a figure below it indicating the number of weapons in the troop (*see* Sec 43).

Section 39.—PLATOONS AND EQUIVALENT UNITS

Platoons are indicated by the company sign as in Sec 38 (a) and (b) above, but without the thickened side.

Sig pl   Tk tp

Section 40.—BASIC SIGNS FOR WEAPONS AND EQUIPMENT

The following is the list of basic signs for weapons and equipment:—

MG (Lt or Med)	Atk Rifle	Flame Thrower	Inf Gun (Lt or Hy)	Mortar	Atk Gun	Smoke Mortar	Smoke Equipment	Gun	Howitzer	Hy Howitzer (Mörser)	AA Gun	Search-light	Balloon barrage

Tank	Assault gun	Armd tp carrier (light or heavy)	"Volkswagen"	Armd Car (light or heavy)

SECTION 41.—SUPPLEMENTARY SIGNS, LETTERS, AND NUMBERS

The following is the list of supplementary signs, letters and numbers, used in conjunction with the appropriate basic sign to indicate a particular type of weapon or equipment:—

(a) *Supplementary signs indicating method of transport*

Supplementary signs.	Tractor drawn	SP	Ski	Sledge	Railway	Mountain
Examples	AA Gun (tractor drawn)	How (SP)			Ry AA Gun	Mtn Inf Gun
					E on right of basic sign.	

(b) *Supplementary signs indicating gun positions*

Supplementary signs.	In position	In fixed position	Gun in fixed position	In fixed position under armour or concrete *Under construction*	*Completed*
Examples	Atk gun in position		Gun in fixed position	How in fixed position under armour or concrete	

SECTION 42.—OTHER SUPPLEMENTARY SIGNS USED WITH BASIC GUN SIGNS

	Origin	Calibre	No. of guns	Range	Barrage Tp
Supplementary letters and numbers	On right of basic sign b—Belgian j—Yugoslav d—Danish n—Norwegian e—English ö—Austrian f—French p—Polish h—Dutch r—Russian t—Czech	Figures on left of sign Or letters on left of sign as follows:— le=leicht=light or field m=mittel=medium s=schwer=medium or heavy sw=schwerst=superheavy Short and long guns of the same calibre are differentiated by the letters k (=kurz), and l (=lang) respectively on the right of the figures showing calibre or number of guns.	Figure below sign Where within a unit there are weapons of the same type but of different calibres, one basic sign may be used to indicate all the weapons, the numbers of each type being given below it, commencing with the highest calibre on the left. *Examples:* 2+6 3+0+6 Two 15-cm Three 12-cm (5·91-in) and (4·71-in) and six 7·5-cm six 5-cm (2-in) (2·95-in) mortars infantry guns	Figure in kms over sign	Sp on left of sign below calibre
	"Home Guard" AA Hei on right of sign under origin	"Emergency" AA Al on right of sign under origin	AA	Service	
				Army: H—Black Navy: M—Blue Air Force: L—Green Letter in brackets next to unit No. on right of sign *Or* unit No. in colours shown	

Section 43.—EXAMPLES OF COMBINATION OF BASIC GUN SIGNS WITH SUPPLEMENTARY SIGNS

Army Hy SP Gun Tp with French guns	Naval Super Hy Gun Tp in fixed position under concrete	Air Force Hy " Emergency " AA Tp in position
20·9 2/109(H) f 19·4 3	40·6, 56 (M) 3	8·8 1/22(L) 4 A1
Range=20·9 km No. of Guns=3 Calibre=19·4 cm Unit=2 Tp 109 AR Origin=French	Range=56 km No. of Guns=3 Calibre=40·6 cm	No. of Guns=4 Calibre = 8·8 cm Unit=1 Tp 22 AA Regt

Section 44.—SUPPLEMENTARY SIGNS FOR TYPES OF AFV

Tanks

Types of tanks are indicated by Roman numerals within the basic tank sign, thus :—

Pz Kw IV = [IV]

NOTE.—It is expressly laid down that the abbreviations " le ", " m ", etc., must not be used with the basic tank sign to indicate particular types of tank. These abbreviations may, however, be used to indicate tank units, thus light tank squadron = [le]

ACV : An ACV is indicated thus :—

The following is a selection of signs for field defences, which may be found on German maps. Here again German practice is not consistent and alternative signs may be used, with or without an explanatory legend.

	Wire fence
	Belt of wire with double-apron
	Wire netting obstacle
	Trip-wire
	Plain and barbed wire concertina
	Demolitions, prepared
	Demolitions, fired
	Field of buried anti-tank mines
	Field of surface anti-tank mines
	Field of crushing plant mines
	Anti-personnel minefield
	Hasty telegraph and pressure obstacle
	Improvised hasty obstacle
	Area sown with improvised mines (all types)
	Electrified wire obstacle
	Felled tree obstacle, light
	Felled tree obstacle, heavy
	Belt of felled trees
	Road block-works, M.T., ploughs, earthworks, agricultural and industrial machinery, etc.
	As above, with gap for admitting traffic
	Wire rope obstacle
	Steel rail or girder obstacle
	Stake obstacle
	Anti-tank ditch
	Dam
	Culvert with penstock
	Land artificially flooded (colouring in blue)
	Felled woodland, demolished farm buildings
	Terrain naturally tank-proof
	Contaminated belts (hachuring in yellow) individual areas of contamination (hachuring in yellow)
	Bats rendered impassable by fire (hachuring in red)

Note: Dummy obstacles are indicated by the letters Sch (=Scheinsperre)

Section 46.—BOUNDARIES

The following are the signs usually used for boundaries :—

Div	Regt	Bn (or equivalent)
⊢ ⊢ ⊢	— .. — .. —	.—.—.—.—.—.—.—

Coy (or equivalent)	Objective	Limit of Recce
— — — — — —	....	+—+—+—+—+—+—+

SECTION 47.—TYPES OF AIRCRAFT AND GAF FLYING FORMATIONS AND UNITS

The following table gives the new signs for types of aircraft and GAF flying formations and units :—

BASIC SIGNS	Long Distance Recce	Army Co-operation	Bomber	Dive Bomber	Twin Engine Fighter	Single Engine Fighter	Night Fighter	Ground Attack	Transport	Multi-Purposes	Courier
Aerial Torpedo			LT								
Fighter Bomber						Bo					
Tank Buster					Pz						
Railway Destruction						Eisb					
High Altitude	Hö		Hö			Hö					
Coastal (Land A/C)	Kü		Kü		Kü						
Naval Aircraft											
Ship borne Aircraft		Bd									
Carrier Borne A/C				Trg		Trg				Trg	

Supplementary Signs

FORMATIONS AND UNITS											
	Single Engine Fighter Wing		HQ Single Engine Fighter Wing		HQ Bomber Group	HQ Bomber Group		Bombers (12 AC)		Ground Attack (41 AC)	

PART V.—EQUIPMENT

TANKS

TABLE 63

	Pz Kw II (Sd Kfz 121)	Pz Kw III (Sd Kfz 141)	Pz Kw IV (Sd Kfz 161)	Pz Kw VI (H)—Tiger
Weight	9½ tons	22 tons	23 tons	56 tons
Crew	3	5	5	5
Dimensions:				
1. Length... ...	15 ft 3 in	17 ft 9 in	19 ft 4 in	20 ft 6 in
2. Width	7 ft 4 in	9 ft 8 in	9 ft 7 in	10 ft 6 in (narrow tracks) 11 ft 9 in (wide tracks)
3. Height	6 ft 6 in	8 ft 3 in	8 ft 6 in	9 ft 6 in
4. Belly clearance	1 ft 1 in	1 ft 3 in	1 ft 3 in	1 ft 4 in
Armour:				
1. Front	15 mm+20 mm=35 mm	50 mm+20 mm (spaced) =70 mm	50 mm	102 mm
2. Sides	15 mm	30 mm	30 mm	82 mm
3. Top	10–15 mm	12 mm	12 mm	26 mm
Armament:				
1. Turret	One 2-cm (·79-in) KwK 30 or 38, and One 7·92-mm (·31-in) MG 34 coaxial.	One long 5-cm (1·97-in) KwK 39 or One short 7·5-cm (2·95-in) KwK and One 7·92-mm (·31-in) MG 34 coaxial.	One long 7·5-cm (2·95-in) KwK 40 and One 7·92-mm (·31-in) MG 34 coaxial.	One long 8·8-cm (3·46-in) KwK 36 and One 7·92-mm (·31-in) MG 34 coaxial.
2. Hull	NONE	One 7·92-mm (·31-in) MG 34.	One 7·92-mm (·31-in) MG 34.	One 7·92-mm (·31-in) MG 34.
Engine	140 hp 6 cyl petrol, water-cooled.	300 hp 12 cyl petrol, water-cooled.	300 hp 12 cyl petrol, water-cooled.	640 hp 12 cyl petrol, water-cooled.

TABLE 63—*contd.*

TANKS—*contd.*

	Pz Kw II (Sd Kfz 121)	Pz Kw III (Sd Kfz 141)	Pz Kw IV (Sd. Kfz 161)	Pz Kw VI (H)—Tiger
Drive	Front sprocket	Front sprocket	Front sprocket	Front sprocket
Max speed	30 mph	28 mph	25 mph	17 mph
Performance : 1. Trench crossing 2. Step ... ... 3. Water forded ... 4. Max gradient ...	 5 ft 6 in 2 ft 2 ft 6 in 27°	 8 ft 6 in 2 ft 2 ft 9 in 27°	 9 ft 2 ft 2 ft 9 in 30°	 10 ft 2 ft 6 in Submersible to 15 ft 30°
Suspension	Five independently sprung twin-rubber-tyred 22-in diameter bogie-wheels. Four return rollers.	Six 20-in diameter rubber-tyred bogie-wheels sprung on torsion bars.	Eight 18½-in diameter rubber tyred bogie-wheels in pairs. Quarter elliptic springs. Four return rollers.	Large overlapping rubber tyred bogie wheels sprung on torsion bars. Eight bogie wheels visible each side, four of which partly obscure the other four.
Communication ...	WT, RT, flag.	WT, RT, flag, intercomn phone.	WT, RT, flag, intercomn phone.	WT, RT, flag, intercomn phone.
Remarks	An alternative type with four large bogie-wheels each side touching top and bottom of tracks mounts 2 flame-throwers and 1 MG as armament, but this type is rare.	Radius of action—108 miles (roads), 58 miles (cross-country).	Radius of action—130 miles (roads) 80 miles (cross-country)	

TABLE 64

ARMOURED CARS

Type	Light 4-wheeled armoured car Sd Kfz 222	Heavy 8-wheeled armoured car Sd Kfz 231 (8 Rad)
Weight	4·7 tons	8 tons
Crew	3	4
Dimensions :		
Length	15 ft 7 in	21 ft (incl spaced shield)
Width	6 ft 6 in	7 ft 3 in
Height	6 ft	7 ft 10 in
Ground clearance	10 in	9 in
Armour :		
Front...	8 mm	8+10 mm* (spaced)=18 mm
Sides	8 mm	8 mm
Top	6 mm	5 mm
†*Armament*	One 2-cm (·79-in) KwK 30 or 38 and one 7·92-mm (·31-in) MG 34, co-axial in turret	One 2-cm (·79-in) KwK 30 or 38 and one 7·92-mm (·31-in) MG 34, co-axial in turret ‡
Max speed—mph	30 (roads); 20 (cross-country)	50 (roads)
Radius of action—miles ...	180 (roads); 110 (cross-country)	250 (roads)
Communication	WT or RT and flag	WT and flag

NOTES.—* A 10-mm V-shield is mounted about 2 ft in front of the nose of the hull which is 8-mm thick.

† All crews of armoured cars are armed with machine carbines, probably on a scale of 2 per vehicle.

‡ A model of the 8-wheeled armoured car mounting a short 7·5 cm tank gun in an open fighting compartment will also be encountered.

TABLE 65

ARTILLERY WEAPONS—MOUNTAIN, FIELD, MEDIUM, AND HEAVY

Type	Weight in action	Weight of shell	Muzzle velocity—feet per sec	Maximum range—yds	Degrees elevation	Degrees depression	Degrees traverse	Remarks
5-cm (2·95-in) mountain gun (Geb K15)	·62 tons	12 lb	Normal third charge—1,000 Super fourth—1,270	5,890 7,250	50°	−9°	7°	Obsolescent equipment
5-cm (2·95-in) mountain gun (Geb Gesch 36)	·74 tons	HE—12 lb 10 oz or 12 lb 13 oz Hollow charge shell—9 lb 12 oz	1,558 (HE) 1,280 (hollow charge)	10,115 (HE) 1,094 (hollow charge shell)	70°	−1° 53'	40° (trails open) 4° (trails closed)	Indicator shell (K Gr rot Deut für Geb G36)
5-cm (2·95-in) light field gun (lFK18)	1·1 tons	13 lb (HE) 13·6 lb (smoke) 11 lb (hollow charge) 15 lb (APCBC tracer)	590 (small charge) 1,180 (medium charge) 1,590 (large charge)	2,980 8,070 10,310	45°	−5°	30°	Very light equipment, on wooden spoked artillery wheels; but travels well behind a fast truck
0·5-cm (4·14-in) guns (s10 cm K18)	5·5 tons	33·5 lb (HE) 31·25 lb (AP) 34·62 lb (APCBC)	1,805 (small charge) 2,264 (medium charge) 2,740 (large charge)	13,900 (small) 17,200 (medium) 20,800 (large)	45°	−1°	60°	Standard equipment. Being replaced by 10-cm K42
0·5-cm (4·14-in) gun howitzer (lFH18, and lFH18M)	1·9 tons	32·6 lb (HE) 31·25 lb (AP tracer) 25·9 lb (hollow charge) 32·4 lb and 30·8 lb (smoke shell)	Normal fifth charge—1,280 Super sixth charge—1,540	11,670	40°	−6°	56°	lFH18M fitted with muzzle brakes, fires a special long range shell with long range charge. MV=1,772 f/sec. Max range=13,470 yds. An lFH42 has also been reported
0·5-cm (4·14-in) mountain howitzer (Geb H40)								
5-cm (5·91-in) howitzer (sFH18)	5·4 tons	95·7 lb (HE anti-concrete shell, AP shell, smoke shell)	1,705	14,570	45°	−1°	60°	A model with muzzle brake, sFH 18/40, has been reported, also an sFH42 details of which are not known
5-cm (5·91-in) gun (K16)	10·7 tons	113·5 lb (HE)	2,485 (large) 2,280 (medium) 1,820 (small)	24,100	42°	−3°	8°	Believed to be still standard equipment. Improved 15-cm K16 KP of last war
5-cm (5·91-in) gun (K18)	12·6 tons	99 lb (HE APCB and APCBC)	2,920	27,200	45°	−4°	60°	Believed to be new equipment to replace K16. This gun is also provided with a platform weighing 5·9 tons
7·25-cm (6·79-in) medium gun (17-cm K18 in Mrs Lafette)	17·5 tons	150 lb (charge 1-3) 138 lb (charge 4)	2,034 2,428 2,821 3,035	20,013 32,371	50°	0°	16° (360° on platform)	Carriage interchangeable with 21-cm Mrs18. Can be used against AFVs at ranges up to 1,640 yds
1-cm (8·27-in) howitzer (Lg 21-cm Mrs)	9 tons	264 lb	1,350	11,220	70°	6°	4°	Obsolete equipment
1-cm (8·27-in) howitzer (Mörser 18)	16·4 tons	267 lb (HE—21-cm Gr18) (Anti-concrete—21-cm Gr 18 Be)	1,854	18,263	72°	0°	360°	New equipment

ARTILLERY WEAPONS—ANTI-AIRCRAFT

TABLE 66

Type	Calibre	Muzzle velocity in f/s	Max horizontal range yds	Ceiling* ft	Time of flight to ceiling secs	Wt of projectile	Rate of fire		Wt in action	Remarks
							Theoretical	Practical		
2-cm Flak 30	20 mm (·79-in)	2,950	5,230	7,215	6·0	4·2 oz (HE) 5·2 oz (AP)	280	120	9·25 cwt	AA/A tk. Fitted with Flakvisier 35 (course and speed sight). MT drawn or on SP mounting. Accurate engagement unlikely above about 3,500 ft.
2-cm Flak 38	20 mm (·79-in)	2,950	5,230	7,215	6·0	4·2 oz (HE) 5·2 oz (AP)	420–480	180–220	8 cwt	(a) AA/A tk. Fitted with Flakvisier 38 (tachymetric sight). MT drawn or on SP mounting. Accurate engagement unlikely above about 3,500 ft. (b) A mountain version also exists.
2-cm Flakvierling 38 (four-barrelled)	20 mm (·79-in)	2,950	5,230	7,215	6·0	4·2 oz (HE) 5·2 oz (AP)	1680–1920	700–800	1·48 tons	AA/A tk. Fitted with Flakvisier 40 (tachymetric sight). MT drawn or on SP mounting. Accurate engagement unlikely above about 3,500 ft.
3·7-cm Flak 18 & 36	37 mm (1·45·in)	2,690	7,080	13,775	14	1·4 lb (HE) 1·5 lb (AP)	140	60	1·53 tons	(a) AA/A tk. Fitted with Flakvisier 33 (course and speed sight). MT drawn or on SP mounting. There is also a new type shell self-destroying at 7–10 secs at 9,185–11,480 ft. Accurate engagement unlikely above about 5,000 ft. (b) A new gun, the 3·7-cm Flak 37, with identical performance and fitted with Flakvisier 37 (tachymetric sight) has recently been introduced. (c) There is also a 3·7-cm Flak 43, about which nothing is known at present.
8·8-cm Flak 18 & 36	88 mm (3·46-in)	2,690	16,200	32,500	—	20 lb (HE) 21 lb (AP)	—	15–20	4·92 tons	AA/A tk. Telescopic sight, ZF20E, fitted for engagement of ground targets. MT drawn. Effective ceiling: 26,250 ft (see note).
8·8-cm Flak 41	88 mm (3·46-in)	3,280	22,000	39,400	—	20·68 lb (HE) 22·44 lb (AP)	—	20		AA/A tk. MT drawn. Particulars of this gun are at present incomplete. Effective ceiling is estimated at about 35,000 ft (see note).

*NOTE.—Ceilings quoted for *light guns* denote heights at which self-destruction takes place at maximum QE; heights up to which accurate engagement is likely are given in " Remarks " column.
Ceilings quoted for *heavy guns* are based on maximum fuze range; effective ceilings (based on 20 secs engagement of directly approaching aircraft flying at 300 m.p.h. last round being fired at QR 70°) are given in " Remarks " column.

ANTI-TANK AND TANK GUNS

Serial	Type of Weapon	Practical rate of fire rpm	Weight of gun in action	Weight of Projectile	Types of Ammunition and Penetration Performance	Ft per sec Muzzle Velocity	Comments
1	2-cm (·79-in) AA/A tk gun (2-cm Flak 30)	120	1,036 lb	1. HE 4·2 oz 2. AP 5·2 oz 3. AP incendiary 5·2 oz 4. AP 40 shot 3·6 oz	HE incendiary (with or without tracer), AP, AP incendiary, AP self-destroying and AP 40 shot. The AP shell penetrates 31 mm of homogeneous armour plate at 30° at 100 yds and 25 mm at 30° at 400 yds. The AP 40 shot penetrates 49 mm at 30° at 100 yds and 37 mm at 400 yds.	1. 2950 2. 2625 3. 2625 4. 3270 (AP 40)	MT drawn or on SP mounting.
2	2-cm (·79-in) AA/A tk gun four-barrelled (2-cm Flakvierling 38)	700–800	1·48 tons	See Serial No. 1	See Serial No. 1	See Serial No. 1	Four 2-cm Flak 38 guns mounted together with a dual AA/A tk role. Normally transported on Trailer 52 (Sd Ah 52), but is also carried on semi-tracked vehicles. Provision is made for single shot or continuous fire on each weapon.
3	2-cm (·79-in) AA/A tk gun (2-cm Flak 38)	180–220	906 lbs, but in draught is about 14¾ cwt	See Serial No. 1	See Serial No. 1	See Serial No. 1	This is the single version of the Flakvierling 38 above. The performance of the gun does not differ materially from the older 2-cm Flak 30 apart from a higher rate of fire. There is a mtn version (2-cm Geb Flak 38), exactly the same, but on a light mounting—7 cwt.
4	2-cm (·79-in) Tank gun (2-cm KwK 30)	120	Weight of gun 142·5 lb	See Serial No. 1	See Serial No. 1	See Serial No. 1	The piece is the same as the 2-cm Flak 30 (Serial No. 1 above). It was formerly the principal armament of the Pz Kw II and stands in a similar relationship to the later 2-cm KwK 38 as does the 2-cm Flak 30 to the 2-cm Flak 38.

No.	Designation	Rds per min	Weight of gun	Weight of projectile	Performance	M.V. (f.s.)	Remarks
5	2-cm (·79-in) Tank gun (2-cm KwK 38)	180–220	Weight of gun 142·5 lb	See Serial No. 1	See Serial No. 1	See Serial No. 1	This gun is essentially identical in design with the 2-cm Flak 38, save that the magazine holds only 10 rds against 20 in the case of the 2-cm Flak 38. It is the latest model of the 2-cm KwK 30, whose functions it assumed.
6	2·8-cm (1·1-in) A tk gun 41 (2·8-cm Pz B 41)	8 to 10	501 lb	AP 4·6 oz HE 3·02 oz	HE and AP. The AP shell penetrates 69 mm of homogeneous armour plate at 100 yds at 30° and 53 mm at 30° at 400 yds	AP 4580	Tapered-bore gun. Splits up into loads of under 132 lb. Normally it is towed portee on a lorry, split into a five-man load or transported by air. There is also a specially light parachutists' version.
7	3·7-cm (1·45-in) A tk gun (3·7-cm Pak)	8 to 10	890 lb	1. HE 1 lb 6 oz (shell) 2 lb 10 oz (round) 2. AP 1 lb 8 oz (shell) 3 lb 2 oz (round) 3. AP 40 shot 12·5 oz 2 lb 4. 3·7-cm (1·45-in) muzzle stick bomb (Mun 3·7-cm Pak Stiel Gr) 13 lb.	HE, AP and AP 40 shot. AP penetrates 42 mm of homogeneous armour plate at 200 yds at 30°, 36 mm at 500 yds at 30°. AP 40 shot penetrates 68 mm at 100 yds at 30°, 49 mm at 400 yds at 30°	AP 2,625 AP 40 3,450	This was formerly the chief German anti-tank gun, but is now being extensively replaced by the 5-cm (1·97-in) A tk gun 38. It is towed on its own wheels, or mounted in an armd tp carrying vehicle and can be air-borne.
8	4·2-cm (1·65-in) A tk gun (4·2-cm Pak 41)			AP ·796 lb	AP estimated penetration 93 mm homogeneous armour plate at 30° at 200 yds, 55 mm at 30° at 1,000 yds. HE also fired.	4,600	Tapered-bore gun.
9	4·7-cm (1·85-in) SP A tk gun (4·7-cm Pak)	12	7·5 tons complete with chassis	1. HE 5·1 lb 2. AP 3·6 lb 3. AP 40 1·8 lb	AP, HE and AP 40. AP penetrates 59 mm of homogeneous armour plate at 30° at 300 yds, 55 mm at 500 yds and 47 mm at 1,000 yds at 30°.	AP 2,540 HE 1,300	Mounted on the Pz Kw I tk chassis, and has a three-sided armour plate shield. With the gun are 74 rounds AP and 10 rounds HE. The gun itself is of Czech origin. It has a crew of three.
10	5-cm (1·97-in) A tk gun (5-cm Pak 38)		2,016 lb (18 cwt)	1. HE 3·9 lb 2. APC 4·56 lb 3. AP 40 2 lb	APC penetrates 65 mm of homogeneous armour plate at normal at 500 yds, and 52 mm at 1,000 yds at 30°. Fires HE, APC, and AP 40.	APC 2,700 AP 40 3,445 HE 1,800	Mounted on a split trail carriage and normally towed by a semi-tracked tractor. Can be air-transported.
11	5-cm (1·97-in) Tk gun (5-cm KwK)		Weight of gun, 489 lb	1. HE 3·9 lb 2. APC 4·56 lb 3. AP 40 2 lb	Fires HE, APC and AP 40. APC penetrates 68 mm of homogeneous armour plate at normal at 500 yds and 54 mm at 1,200 yds. AP 40 shot penetrates 83 mm of homogeneous armour plate at 30° at 200 yds, and 69 mm at 500 yds.	APC 2,250 AP 40 3,445 HE 1,476	Mounted in the older Pz Kw III tank.

TABLE 67—contd.

ANTI-TANK AND TANK GUNS—contd.

Serial	Type of Weapon	Practical rate of fire rpm	Weight of gun in action	Weight of Projectile	Types of Ammunition and Penetration Performance	Ft per sec Muzzle Velocity	Comments
12	5-cm (1·97-in) Tk gun in later Pz Kw IIIs (5-cm KwK 39, formerly known as the KwKL/60)		Weight of gun 672 lb	As serial 10 above	As serial 10 above	As serial 10 above	This long gun is virtually identical with the 5-cm Pak 38. It has, however, no muzzle brake and it is fired electrically instead of by percussion. It is fitted into the newer types of Pz Kw III.
13	7·5-cm (2·95-in) Tank gun (short) (7·5-cm KwK)		628 lb but when on assault chassis total weight is 20 tons	1. HE 12·56 lb 2. APCBC 14·8 lb 3. Smoke 14 lb 4. Hollow charge 9·87 lb	Fires HE, APCBC, Smoke and Hollow charge. The APCBC penetrates 46 mm of homogeneous armour plate at 30° at 500 yds, 41 mm at 1,000 yds and 40 mm at 1,200 yds.	APCBC 1,350	This gun is electrically fired. It is mounted in the old Pz Kw IV tank, some of the newer Pz Kw III tanks and eight-wheeled armd cars, and the 7·5-cm "short" tank gun. As an assault gun it is known as the Stu G 7·5-cm K and is mounted in a Pz Kw III chassis. The gun compartment is roofed over, and there is a crew of four.
14	7·5-cm (2·95-in) Tank gun (long) (7·5-cm KwK 40)			1. HE 12 lb 10 oz 2. APCBC 15 lb 3. AP 40 7 lb 1 oz 4. Hollow charge: i. 9 lb 12 oz ii. 10 lb 2 oz.	Fires HE, APCBC, hollow charge and AP 40. APCBC penetrates 89 mm of homogeneous armour plate at 30° at 500 yds, 79 mm at 1,000 yds, and 62 mm at 2,000 yds	APCBC 2,526 HE 1,800 Hollow charge 1,476	This is the "long" version of the 7·5-cm tk gun. It is, to a large extent, replacing the short 7·5-cm KwK. It is mounted in the newer Pz Kw IV tanks, and as an assault gun is known as the 7·5-cm Stu K 40. It is electrically fired.
15	7·5-cm (2·95-in) A tk gun (7·5-cm Pak 40)		9 cwt	1. HE 12 lb 10 oz 2. APCBC 15 lb 3. AP 40 7 lb 1 oz 4. Hollow charge: 9 lb 12 oz 10 lb 2 oz	HE, APCBC, AP 40, and hollow charge. The APCBC penetrates 112·5-mm of homogeneous armour plate at normal at 500 yds, 102 mm at 1,000 and 82 mm at 2,000 yds	HE 1,800 APCBC 2,830 Hollow charge 1,476	There are three versions of mounting, one being a field mounting which is very like that of the 5-cm Pak 38 above. The other mountings are self-propelled, one on the Pz Kw II chassis and known as the 7·5-cm Pak 40 auf Pz Kw II, and the second on the Czech Pz Kw 38 chassis and known as the 7·5-cm Pak 40 auf Pz Kw 38 (t).
16	7·5-cm (2·95-in) A tk gun (7·5-cm Pak 41)		1·4 tons	5·68 lb, whole round is 16·65 lb	HE (7·5-cm Spgr Patr 41 Pak 41). AP (7·5-cm Pzgr Patr 41 Pak 41). Penetrates 146 mm of homogeneous armour plate at 500 yds at 30°, 130 mm at 1,000 yds, and 114 mm at 1,500 yds	AP 3,936	A long, low, sturdy tapered bore gun drawn by MT. Solid rubber tyres.

No.	Designation	Weight		Ammunition	Performance	Muzzle velocity (f.s.)	Remarks
17	7·5-cm (2·95-in) A tk gun (7·5-cm Pak 97/38)	1·23 tons		HE Hollow charge APCBC	HE, APCBC and hollow charge. Estimated penetration performance is 60 mm homogeneous armour plate at 30° at 900 yds. Types HE:— 233/1 (F) Frz. 17 ; 230/1 (F) " ,900 ; 231/1 (F) " 15 ; 236/1 (F) " 18 } 7·5-cm Spr. / 7·5-cm Gr. Pat	HE 1,892 Hollow charge 1,476	The well-known 75-mm French model 97 gun mounted on a 5-cm Pak 38 carriage and fitted with a muzzle brake.
18	7·62-cm (3-in) A tk gun (7·62-cm Pak 36 (r))	1·7 tons		1. HE 12·6 lb 2. AP 40 9·2 lb 3. APCBC 16·7 lb	APCBC penetrates 94 mm at 30° at 500 yds, 83 mm at 1,000 yds and 64 mm at 2,000 yds	APCBC 2,430 AP 40 3,520 HE 1,805	This gun is towed on its own wheels. It is also mounted on a Pz Kw II chassis, known as 7·62-cm Pak 36 (r) auf Pz Kw II, on a Pz Kw 38 (t) chassis (Czech) or on semi-tracked vehicles. Its crew probably numbers six.
19	8·8-cm (3·46-in) Multi-purpose gun (8·8-cm Flak 18 and 36)	4·92 tons	15 to 20	1. HE 20 lb 2. APCBC 21 lb 3. AP 40 4. Hollow charge	HE with time fuze, HE with percussion fuze and APCBC. The APCBC penetrates 110 mm of homogeneous armour plate at normal at 500 yds, 101 mm at 1,000, 92 mm at 1,500, and 87 mm at 2,000 yds	HE 2,690 AP 2,600	This multi-purpose gun is MT drawn on Trailer 201, from which it can engage ground targets, after detachment from the Sd Kfz 7 (8 ton medium semi-tracked vehicle) which tows it. It is also used on a railway mounting.
20	8·8-cm (3·46-in) KwK 36 tank gun (8·8-cm KwK 36)	4·92 tons	15 to 20	1. HE 20 lb 2. APCBC 21 lb 3. AP 40	As above	As serial 19 above	This gun is virtually identical with the 8·8-cm Flak 36 save that it has electric firing mechanism. Mounted on Pz Kw VI, also as SP A tk gun on Pz Kw VI chassis.
21	8·8-cm (3·46-in) Multi-purpose gun (8·8-cm Flak 41)		20	HE 20·68 lb APCBC 22·45 lb	HE with time or percussion fuzes and APCBC. The APCBC is estimated to penetrate 175 mm of homogeneous armour plate at 500 yds, 164 mm at 1,000 yds, 142 mm at 2,000 yds, and 132 mm at 2,500 yds, all at normal impact.	HE 3,280 AP 3,214	This gun is a much improved version of the 8·8-cm Flak 36. The barrel is nearly 3 ft longer. The APCBC shell is 1¼ lb heavier. The round is electrically fired.

CLOSE-SUPPORT GUNS

TABLE 68

Type	Calibre	Weight	Practical rate of fire rpm	Maximum practical range—yards	Weight of projectile	German name of ammunition fired	Muzzle velocity fs	Remarks
INFANTRY GUNS								
(a) 7·5-cm (2·95-in) inf gun		880 lb	5–10	3,880 / 3,780	12 lb / 13·2 lb	7·5-cm Igr 18 / Do. do.	730 / 690	
(b) 15-cm (5·91-in) inf gun		1·5 tons	4	5,140	83·6 lb	15-cm Igr 33 and 38	790	
ASSAULT GUNS								
(a) 7·5-cm (2·95-in) assault gun		19·9 tons		6,758 / 5,668 / 1,635 / 3,270	12·6 lb / 9·68 lb / 14·96 lb / 13·64 lb	HE / Hollow charge / APCBC, / Smoke	1,378 / 1,476 / 1,263 / 1,387	On Pz Kw III chassis
(b) 15-cm (5·91-in) assault gun		11 tons	4	5,140	83·6 lb	15-cm Igr 33 and 38	790	On Pz Kw II chassis

TABLE 69

INFANTRY WEAPONS

Type	Calibre	Weight	Practical rate of fire rpm	Maximum practical range yards	Weight of projectile	German name of ammunition fired	Muzzle velocity f.s.	Remarks
Pistols								
(a) Pistol 08 (Lüger) ...	9 mm (·35")	1 lb 14 oz	—	50 to 100 yds	123 grains	Pist Patr 08 (ball)		Self-loading — One of the standard service pistols.
(b) Pistol 38 (Walther) ...	9 mm (·35")	1 lb 15 oz	—	50 to 100 yds	123 grains	Pist Patr 08 (ball)		Self-loading. Another standard pistol.
(c) Grenade pistol (Walther) (Kampfpistole)	27 mm (1")	1 lb 9¼ oz	—	100 yds (approx)	5 oz	{ Sprenggranate Z (HE) Nebelgranate Z (smoke) Deutgranate Z (indicating)		A modification of a standard signal pistol with a rifled barrel and small dial sight.
Rifles								
(a) Rifle 98 (bolt-operated) ...	7·92 mm (·31")	About 9 lb	—	Sighted for 100–200 metres	198 grains 194 grains	Patr SS (ball) Patr Sm K (H) (AP with tungsten carbide core)	2,510 2,860	Several types in use, the latest being a short rifle (length 44¼ in) Gewehr 98/40.
(b) Rifle 41 (W) (self-loading)	7·92 mm (·31")	10 lb 14 oz	—	Sighted for 100–1,200 metres	,,	,,	,,	Reload automatically after each shot. Magazines hold 10 rounds.
(c) Rifle 41 (M) (self-loading)	7·92 mm (·31")	10 lb 4 oz	—	,,	,,	,,	,,	
Rifle-grenades (fired from discharger cup fitted to rifle (a) or anti-tank rifle (b))								
(a) Anti-personnel	3-cm (1·2")	9 oz	10–15	250	9 oz	Gewehr Spreng-granate 30	—	(a) Can be thrown by hand, with 4½ sec delay. Functions when fired on impact; self-destroying after 11 sec should fuze not function.
(b) Small anti-tank	3-cm (1·2")	8·8 oz	,,	100	8·8 oz	Gewehr Panzer-granate 30	—	Functions on impact on hollow charge principle. Penetration approx 30 mm.
(c) Large anti-tank	3-cm (1·2")	13·5 oz	,,	100	13·5 oz	Gross Gewehr Panzergranate 40	—	Has a larger bursting charge than (b).
Hand grenades								
(a) Stick grenade	—	{1 lb 5 oz {1 lb 6 oz	—	About 50	{1 lb 5 oz {1 lb 6 oz	—	—	There are two types, model 24 and PH 39. HE may be replaced by smoke composition, and in this case is sometimes fitted with an adaptor for throwing without the stick.
(b) Egg grenade	—	8 or 10 oz	—	About 25	8 or 10 oz	—	—	Relies on blast for effect as (a) above. 5 sec delay.
Anti-tank rifles								
(a) A tk rifle (Pz B 39) ...	7·92 mm (·31")	27 lb 4 oz	6–8	Up to 300 yds	225 grains	Patr 318	3,800 (approx)	Fires an AP tracer bullet with a tungsten carbide core and a small lachrymatory pellet. Penetration 33 mm at 100 yds at normal.
(b) A tk grenade rifle (Granatbüchse 39)	7·92 mm (·31")	23 lb 2 oz	—	—	—	—	—	Fitted with discharger cup and fires rifle grenades described above. Bulleted blank cartridge.

TABLE 69—contd.

INFANTRY WEAPONS—contd.

Type	Calibre	Weight	Practical rate of fire rpm	Maximum practical range yards	Weight of projectile	German name of ammunition fired	Muzzle velocity f.s.	Remarks
Machine carbines Schmeisser MP38/40 … …	9 mm (·35″)	9 lb	Cyclic 520–540	Up to 250–300 yds	123 grains 98·5 grains	Pist Patr 08 (ball) Pist Patr 08 m.E. (semi-AP)	1,260	The standard weapon. Vertical box magazine 32 rds. The following other types are in service: (a) Schmeisser 28t. Straight box magazine in left side of weapon—32 rds. (b) Bergmann MP18t. Snail type magazine on left side. (c) Bergmann MP34t. Straight box magazine on right. (d) Steyr-Solothurn MP34 (ö). Straight box magazine on left. Fires long Mauser pistol ammunition (Pist Patr M 34 (ö)).
Machine guns (a) MG 34 … … …	7·92 mm (·31″)	26·5 lb (weight tripod 42 lb)	150 as MMG 300 (cyclic 800–900)	1,650 as MMG 3,750	198 grains 178 ″ 157 ″	*For LMG* Patr s.S. (ball) Patr s.m.K (A.P.) Patr s.m.K.L'sp (A.P./T)		These MGs may be used as light or medium MGs according to type of mounting provided (bipod or tripod). Belts of 50 are fired and two or more may be joined. Barrel changing after 250 rds more or less continuous fire. Single and twin AA mountings are also provided.
(b) MG 42 … … …	7·92 mm (·31″)	23·75 lb (weight tripod 43¼ lb)	150–160 as MMG probably 400 (cyclic about 1200)	1,650 as MMG 3,750		*For MMG* Patr s.S. or S.m.E. (semi-A.P.) Patr S.m.K. Patr S.m.K.L'sp		
Mortars (a) 5-cm (l.Gr.W.36). (equivalent of 2″)	—	30·8 lb	Max 45	515	2·2 lb	5-cm Wgr 36 (HE)	262	The standard light mortar. Has one charge only.
(b) 8-cm (m.Gr.W.34). (equivalent of 3″)	—	12·5 lb	Max 45	2,078	7·75 lb	8-cm Wgr 34 (HE) ″ ″ 38 (airburst) ″ ″ 39 ″ ″ ″ 34 (Nb)'(smoke) ″ ″ 34 (Dent) (indicator)	499	Divides into three parts, each weighing about 40 lb. The crew consists of one NCO and five men. Has five charges.
(c) 12-cm (4·7″). See Remarks. (ii) Russian ″. (iii) French "Brandt". (iii) Finnish "Tampella".	12-cm (4·7″) 12-cm (4·7″) 12-cm (4·7″)	5¼ cwt 16 cwt 5 cwt	6 6 12	6,500 8,000 7,550	35 lb 37 lb 27¼ lb	(i) 12-cm Wgr 378/1 (r) ″ ″ 378/2 (r) ″ ″ 378/3 (r) all HE	— — —	Certain German units are being equipped with 12-cm mortars. These are certainly the Russian (i) (Gr.W.378 (r), and may also be the French "Brandt" (ii) or the Finnish "Tampella" (iii) 12-cm mortars.

BRIDGING EQUIPMENT

TABLE 70

Type	Where found		Details of Equipment
D Bridging equipment.	Infantry pioneer platoons (mech)	Brückengerät D—light box girder bridge.	Will take loads up to 9 tons and is of the pontoon, trestle and girder type. The girder is 30 ft long.
B Bridging equipment.	Infantry divisional engineer battalions. Some motorized divisional engineer battalions. Some armoured divisional engineer battalions (in addition to the "K" equipment).	Brückengerät B—pontoon and trestle bridge. Bridging columns B normally have two identical platoons (Pontonzüge) to carry main equipment, and a third platoon (Ergänzungszug) with supplementary equipment. Where there is a tank bridgelaying platoon, this is the third platoon and the "Ergänzungszug" becomes the fourth platoon.	Has a normal type superstructure comprising road-bearers, chesses and ribands supported on undecked steel pontoons, which can be used singly or joined together stern to stern to form pontoon piers. Three types of bridge can be built—4, 9 and 18-tons. This last has been recently strengthened to a rating of 20-tons, but its maximum load is probably about 26 tons.
C Bridging equipment.	May still be found in some infantry divisional engineer battalions.	Brückengerät C — an earlier type than B.	The pontoons are smaller than the B type and made of wood. The superstructure is in made-up lengths about 23 ft by 2 ft. Four types of bridge can be built: (i) an assault bridge, single strips supported on single pontoons; (ii) 1-ton bridge, 5 strips wide on double pontoons; (iii) 4-ton bridge, like the 1-ton but with twice as many pontoon piers; (iv) 5·3-ton bridge (to take the 5·3-ton six-wheeled armd car). Each bay is supported on three piers.
K Bridging equipment.	The standard bridge of the engineer battalion in the armoured division.	Brückengerät K—light box girder bridge.	The pontoons are of the three-section type and the superstructure is thought to have been modelled on the British small box girder bridge Mark II; 2, 3 or 4 girders may be used. The full girder is 60 ft. long. Two will carry eight tons, three will carry 16 tons. The official rating of the four-girder bridge is also 16 tons, but will carry at least 24 tons.
LZ Bridge.	Railway engineer battalions.	Semi-permanent heavy bridge of the through-type sectional girder class.	Can be used for spans up to 145 feet. Officially it carries wheeled vehicles up to 18 tons and tracked vehicles up to 30 tons.

BRIDGING EQUIPMENT—contd.

TABLE 70—contd.

Type	Where found	Details of Equipment
Herbert equipment.	In the GHQ pool of engineers.	Semi-permanent heavy bridge, with heavy pontoons and a built-up girder superstructure.	Czech in origin. Spans, unsupported, 82 feet, and will take 20-ton wheeled vehicles and 24-ton tracked vehicles. The pontoons are of metal, decked and divided into sections.
The "Roth Wagner" The "Krupp," The "Kohn," The "Ungarn."	Railway engineers.	Semi-permanent heavy railway bridges, none of recent development.	Of the unit construction type with standard parts which can be used alike in spans and piers.
S Bridging equipment.	In the GHQ pool of engineers.	Semi-permanent heavy pontoon bridge (Brückengerät S) used only for heavy traffic across wide rivers.	The roadway is 16 ft 6 in wide and will accommodate two lines of traffic. The pontoons are sectional. Wheeled vehicles up to 24 tons and tracked vehicles up to 30 tons can be accommodated in single line traffic.
The "Unger."	Probably in the GHQ pool.	Portable tank bridge.	A double track bridge 22 ft long, made of timber, mounted on wheels and said to carry 22 tons.
Improvised bridging material.	All engineer units.	Bridges vary from light timber foot bridges, supported on rubber pneumatic boats, to semi-permanent bridges with a capacity of more than 20 tons.	All engineer companies carry a small supply of timber for this purpose. Apart from the lightest types, bridges are classified as of 2, 4, 8, 16 and 24-ton capacity, the last three being regarded as heavy bridges. These bridges can be constructed on fixed or floating supports. Common to most engineer units are the two standard types of pneumatic rubber boat, which can be used for ferrying, rafting or bridging. These two types are :— (i) large (grosser Flosssack) 18 ft by 6 ft, weight 330 lb, will carry a section of ten in addition to a crew of seven. A pair joined together makes a 2-ton raft. (ii) small (kleiner Flosssack) 10 ft by 4 ft, will carry one man in addition to crew of two ; weight 110 lb. When fitted with a duckboard type of wooden superstructure it forms a light infantry assault bridge (Flosssackschnellsteg), or with a double-tracked superstructure can take motor cycles (Kradschützensteg).

TABLE 71

SPIGOT MORTARS

Type	Weight	Range	Ammunition fired	Where found	Remarks
20-cm (7·9-in)	205 lb	766 yds (with the 46 lb bomb)	46 lb HE bomb (20-cm Wurfgr 40) A smoke bomb (20-cm Wurfgr 40 Nb) Harpoon ammunition (Harpunengeschoss)	Engr weapon, allocation to units not yet known	This is the "leichter Ladungswerfer 40." It is electrically fired and has a dial sight. It is intended for use against minefields, wire, anti-tank obstacles, weapon emplacements. The harpoon ammunition is used to draw prepared charges or mine exploding net (Knallnetz) over wire or minefields.
38-cm (15-in)	Not known	Not known	331 lb HE bomb (38-cm Wurfgr 40) A smoke bomb (38-cm Wurfgr 40 Nb)	Also an engineer weapon allocation to units not yet known	This is the "schwerer Ladungswerfer 40." It is thought to be similar in construction to the 20-cm spigot mortar and to be used in a similar way.

TABLE 72

FLAMETHROWERS

Type	Weight (charged)	Quantity of fuel carried	Range	Duration of continuous discharge	Remarks
	lb.	*gals.*	*yds.*	*secs.*	
Small, model 35	79	2·2	25	10–12	The equipment with which the army was equipped at the outbreak of war. This is a one-man load, though it usually has a crew of two. The equipment is carried on the back. Ignition is by means of a ring of burning hydrogen gas round the nozzle of the projector.
Small, model 40 (Lifebuoy)	47	1·5	25	8	This is a lightweight flamethrower, made in the form of two lifebuoy like rings—a large outer one for fuel and a smaller concentric one for hydrogen. In respects other than the pack layout, this equipment resembles the one above.
Small, model 41	44½	1·5	25	8	This flamethrower has a pack of two horizontal cylinders, the lower (larger) one for fuel and the upper one for nitrogen. The projector is the same as that used in the earlier models, with a long, thin cylinder (for hydrogen) mounted on the top.
Small, model 42	about 42—44	1·5	25	8	The model 42 flamethrower is the same as the model 41 except for the projector, which is a new design. The projector is shorter, has a large trigger lever on the side (instead of a short one on the top) and incorporates a new method of fuel ignition.
Medium	225	6·6	25—30	25	This is carried on a two-wheeled trolley and is simply a larger model of the small portable flamethrower model 35.
Flamethrower tank Pz Kw II (F) Sd Kfz 122.	—	2 × 35	35	3–4 mins	This equipment has two projectors, one on the front of each track guard. Each projector has a 180° traverse from 9 to 3 o'clock.

NOTE.—To assist maintenance in the field, a recharging trolley is provided. This has two tyred wheels, is drawn by two men and carries fuel oil, a cylinder of nitrogen, charged hydrogen cylinders and spare parts. Total weight 680 lb.

TABLE 73

STANDARD MINES

1. S—mine 35 (SMi 35)—anti-personnel, operated by pressure on push igniter, or by pull on one or more trip wires attached to pull igniters, or by electrical means. Contains about 360 ⅜-in steel balls.

Dimensions :—

    Height 5 in.
    Diameter 4 in.
    Weight 9 lb.

The first explosion blows the mine clear of the ground and the second occurs at a height of from 3 ft to 5 ft. Firing pressure about 15 lb.

2. Tellermines

There are four types of Tellermine :—

British designation	German designation
1. TMi 35	TMi 35
2. TMi 35 (steel)	TMi 35 (Stahl)
3. TMi 42	TMi 42
4. TMi 43 (mushroom)	TMi Pilz 43

Dimensions :—

1. TMi 35   ...   Height 3·2 in
    Diameter 12·6 in
    Weight 19·2 lb
    Firing pressure (a) centre 400–420 lb.
    (b) edge   175–220 lb.

2. TMi 35   ...   Height 3·75 in.
(steel)   Diameter 12·5 in.
    Weight 21 lb.
    Firing pressure, not known.

3. TMi 42   ...   Height 4 in.
    Diameter 12·75 in.
    Weight 19·3 lb.
    Firing pressure, **650 lb (approx.)**

4. TMi 43   ...   Height 3·5 in.
(mushroom)   Diameter 12·5 in.
    Weight, approx 18 lb.
    Firing pressure, not known.

SMOKE MORTARS AND MULTIPLE ROCKET PROJECTORS

TABLE 74

N.B.—The smoke mortars, properly so called at Serials 1 and 2, should not be confused with the rocket projectors at Serials 3 and 5 where the term "smoke mortar" is merely a convenient rendering of the misleading German term "Nebelwerfer." All are potential CW weapons.

Serial	Equipment	Weight in action	Weight of projectile	Type of projectile	Max range	Rate of fire	Transport	Remarks
	SMOKE MORTARS							
1	10·5-cm (4·14-in) smoke mortar 35 (10-cm Nebelwerfer 35)	231 lb	16 lb	HE Smoke	3,300 yds	12–15 rpm	2-wheeled handcart	Standard smoke/CW weapon.
2	10·5-cm (4·14-in) smoke mortar 40 (10-cm Nebelwerfer 40)	15–25 cwt	19 lb	HE Smoke	6,780 yds (min range 550 yds)	8–10 rpm	2-wheeled rubber-tyred carriage	Breech-loaded.
3	MULTIPLE ROCKET PROJECTORS 15-cm (5·91-in) smoke mortar 41 (15-cm Nebelwerfer 41 or Werfer 41; formerly Nebelwerfer d)	10½ cwt	71 lb	HE Smoke	6,670 yds	6 rounds every 90 secs	Mounted on pair of rubber-tyred wheels and split trail	Weapon resembles small gun and has six barrels arranged in circle like the chambers of a revolver.
4	15-cm (5·91-in) rocket projector (15-cm DO Gerät 38)		Probably as for Serial 3	Probably as for Serial 3				Equipment, designed for dropping by parachute, comprises bipod and projector frame in form of rectangular metal framework 7–8 ft×6 ft.
5	21-cm (8·26-in) smoke mortar 42 (21-cm Nebelwerfer 42, formerly Nebelwerfer e)		245 lb	HE				A larger version of the 15-cm (5·91-in) smoke mortar 41.
6	Heavy projector 40 (schweres Wurfgerät 40)		183 lb 174 lb	28-cm (11-in) HE 32-cm (12·6-in) incendiary	1,090–2,080 yds 1,090–2,180 yds Indications of development of new projectile said to have range of 6,000 yds	Four HE or incendiary projectiles in rapid succession		Consists of a stand in the form of a wooden ramp, which is transported to firing position and then dismounted for firing.
7	Heavy projector 41 (schweres Wurfgerät 41)		183 lb 174 lb	28-cm (11-in) HE 32-cm (12·6-in) incendiary	Ditto	Ditto		Similar to heavy projector 40, but stand is made of metal.
8	Heavy projector 40 on armoured semi-tracked vehicle (Schwerer Wurfrahmen 40 am mgp Zgkw—Sd Kfz 251)		Ditto	Ditto	Ditto	6 rounds in 10 secs		Consists of six projector frames, mounted on medium armoured semi-tracked vehicle, three on each side. Frames can be elevated, but not traversed.
9	28/32-cm (11/12·6-in) smoke mortar 41 (28/32-cm Nebelwerfer 41)		183 lb 174 lb	28-cm (11-in) HE 32-cm (12·6-in) incendiary				Fires same ammunition as Serials 6, 7 and 8. Possibly multi-barrelled.

I.—INFANTRY DIVISION AND MOUNTAIN DIVISION (PROBABLY)

Unit	Type of Set Used	(Maximum) Range of Set in Km WT	RT	Frequency Range in Kc/s	Power LT volts	HT volts	Remarks
Infantry regt	5 watt transmitter	90	30	950—3,150	4	330	Transmitter/receiver
Infantry battalion	Pack d2	15	4	33,300—38,000	2	180 (2×90)	Transmitter/receiver
Infantry company	Pack d2	15	4	33,300—38,000	2	180 (2×90)	Transmitter/receiver
	R/T set b or c	—	¼ to 1	120,000—158,000?	2-4	Vibrator	Transmitter/receiver
Artillery regt	20 watt d transmitter	50	50	42,100—47,800	12	375	Works with recce aircraft
	Pack b1	25	10	3,000—5,000	2	180 (2×90)	Transmitter/receiver
Artillery battery	Pack b1	25	10	3,000—5,000	2	180 (2×90)	Transmitter/receiver
Artillery troop	Pack f	25	10	4,500—6,700	2	180 (2×90)	Transmitter/receiver
	20 watt b transmitter	10	10	25,000—27,200	12	375	Used by sound ranging unit
Artillery survey unit	Pack b1	25	10	3,000—5,000'	2	180 (2×90)	Transmitter/receiver
	Pack c	25	10	1,500—2,143	2	180 (2×90)	Transmitter/receiver. (Flash spotting)
Anti-tank battalion	30 watt transmitter a	150	50	1,120—3,000	12	400	May have been replaced by the 80 watt set with same frequency range
	Pack b1	25	10	3,000—5,000	2	180 (2×90)	Transmitter/receiver
Anti-tank company	Pack b1	25	10	3,000—5,000	2	180 (2×90)	Transmitter/receiver
Engineer battalion	Pack b1	25	10	3,000—5,000	2	180 (2×90)	Transmitter/receiver
Engineer company	Pack b1	25	10	3,000—5,000	2	180 (2×90)	Transmitter/receiver
Recce unit HQ	5 watt transmitter	90	30	950—3,150	4	330	The 80 watt transmitter (1,120—3,000 Kc/s) may have replaced this set
	100 watt transmitter (possibly)	200	.	200—1,200	12	1,000	Transmitter/receiver
Recce squadron	Pack b1	25	10	3,000—5,000	2	180 (2×90)	Transmitter/receiver
	Pack b1	25	10	3,000—5,000	2	180 (2×90)	Transmitter/receiver

II.—MOTORIZED DIVISION

Unit	Type of Set Used	(Maximum) Range of Set in Km WT	RT	Frequency Range in Kc/s	Power LT volts	HT volts	Remarks
Mech infantry regt	30 watt transmitter a	150	50	1,120—3,000	12	400	May have been replaced with 80 watt set with same frequency range
Mech infantry battalion	Pack b1	15	4	33,300—38,000	2	180 (2×90)	Transmitter/receiver
Mech infantry company	Pack d2	15	4	33,300—38,000	2	180 (2×90)	Transmitter/receiver
Artillery regt	20 watt d transmitter	50	50	42,100—47,800	12	375	For communicating with recce aircraft
	Pack b1	25	10	3,000—5,000	2	180 (2×90)	Transmitter/receiver
Artillery battery	Pack b1	25	10	3,000—5,000	2	180 (2×90)	Transmitter/receiver
Artillery troop	Pack f	25	10	4,500—6,700	2	180 (2×90)	Transmitter/receiver
	20 watt b transmitter	10	10	25,000—27,200	12	375	Used by sound ranging unit
Artillery survey unit	Pack b1	25	10	3,000—5,000	2	180 (2×90)	Transmitter/receiver
	Pack c	25	10	1,500—2,143	2	180 (2×90)	Transmitter/receiver. (Flash spotting)
Anti-tank battalion	30 watt transmitter a	150	50	1,120—3,000	12	400	May have been replaced with 80 watt set with same frequency range
	Pack b1	25	10	3,000—5,000	2	180 (2×90)	Transmitter/receiver
Anti-tank company	Pack b1	25	10	3,000—5,000	2	180 (2×90)	Transmitter/receiver
Engineer battalion	30 watt transmitter a	150	50	1,120—3,000	12	400	May have been replaced by 80 watt set with same frequency range
	Pack b1	25	10	3,000—5,000	2	180 (2×90)	Transmitter/receiver
Engineer company	Pack b1	25	10	3,000—5,000	2	180 (2×90)	Transmitter/receiver
Recce element HQ	100 watt transmitter	200	70	200—1,200	12	1,000	The 80 watt set (1,120—3,000 Kc/s) may have replaced this set
	20 watt transmitter d	50	50	42,100—47,800	12	375	For working with aircraft (recce)
	100 watt transmitter	200	70	200—1,200	12	1,000	May have been replaced by 80 watt set (1,120—3,000 Kc/s)
Recce sqns and coys	30 watt transmitter d	150	50	1,120—3,000	12	400	May have been replaced by 80 watt set (1,120—3,000 Kc/s)
	20 watt transmitter d	50	50	42,100—47,800	12	375	For working with recce aircraft
	Pack b1	25	10	3,000—5,000	2	180 (2×90)	Transmitter/receiver

III.—ARMOURED DIVISION

Unit	Equipment			Frequency range (Kc/s)			Remarks
Panzer grenadier bde	100 watt transmitter	200	70	200—1,200	12	1,000	The 80 watt transmitter may have replaced this set
	30 watt transmitter a	150	50	1,120—3,000	12	400	This set may have been replaced in some cases by 80 watt transmitter with same frequency range
Panzer grenadier regt	30 watt transmitter a	150	50	1,120—3,000	12	400	
Panzer grenadier battalion	Pack d2	15	4	33,300—38,000	2	180 (2×90)	Transmitter/receiver
Panzer grenadier company	Pack d2	15	4	33,300—38,000	2	180 (2×90)	Transmitter/receiver
Artillery regt	20 watt transmitter d	50	50	42,100—47,800	12	375	Works with recce aircraft
	20 watt c (or 10 watt c)	(10)	(8)	(27,200—33,300)	12	375	Either of these sets would be used for working between arty regt and ACVs or tanks
Artillery battery	Pack b1	25	10	3,000—5,000	2	180 (2×90)	Transmitter/receiver
Artillery troop	Pack f	25	10	4,500—6,700	2	180 (2×90)	Transmitter/receiver
	20 watt b transmitter	10	10	25,000—27,200	12	375	Used by arty sound ranging unit
Artillery survey unit	Pack c	25	10	3,000—5,000	2	180 (2×90)	Transmitter/receiver
	Pack c	25	10	1,500—2,143	2	180 (2×90)	Transmitter/receiver. (Flash spotting)
Anti-tank battalion	30 watt transmitter a	150	50	1,120—3,000	12	400	May have been replaced by 80 watt set with same frequency range
	Pack b1	25	10	3,000—5,000	2	180 (2×90)	Transmitter/receiver
Anti-tank company	Pack b1	25	10	3,000—5,000	2	180 (2×90)	Transmitter/receiver
Engineer battalion	30 watt transmitter a	150	50	1,120—3,000	12	400	May have been replaced by 80 watt set with same frequency range
	Pack b1	25	10	3,000—5,000	2	180 (2×90)	Transmitter/receiver
Engineer company	Pack b1	25	10	3,000—5,000	2	180 (2×90)	Transmitter/receiver
Recce element HQ	100 watt transmitter	200	70	200—1,200	12	1,000	May have been replaced with 80 watt transmitter (a)
	20 watt transmitter d	50	50	42,100—47,800	12	375	Works with recce aircraft
Recce sqns and coys	100 watt transmitter	200	70	200—1,200	12	1,000	May have been replaced by the 80 watt transmitter (a)
	30 watt transmitter a	150	50	1,120—3,000	12	400	May have been replaced by 80 watt set with same frequency range
	20 watt transmitter d	50	50	42,100—47,800	12	375	Works with recce aircraft
	Pack b1	25	10	3,000—5,000	2	180 (2×90)	Transmitter/receiver
Tank regiment	100 watt transmitter	200	70	200—1,200	12	1,000	This set may have been replaced by 80 watt set, range 1,120—3000 Kc/s
	30 watt transmitter a	150	50	1,120—3,000	12	400	This set may have been replaced by 80 watt set, range 1,120—3000 Kc/s
	20 watt transmitter c	10	8	27,200—33,300	12	375	ACV set
	20 watt transmitter d	50	50	42,100—47,800	12	375	Works with recce aircraft
	10 watt transmitter	6	4	27,100—33,300	12	350	Tank set
Tank battalion	20 watt transmitter c	10	8	27,200—33,300	12	375	ACV set
	10 watt transmitter	6	4	27,200—33,300	12	350	Tank set
Tank squadron	20 watt transmitter c	10	8	27,200—33,300	12	375	ACV set
	10 watt transmitter	6	4	27,200—33,300	12	350	Tank set
Tank troop	10 watt transmitter	6	4	27,200—33,300	12	350	Tank set
	10 watt transmitter	6	4	27,200—33,300	12	350	Tank set

NOTES.— (i) Apart from powered gliders, gliders in service with the GAF fall into two main categories, assault gliders (*e.g.* the DFS 230) and freight carrying gliders (*e.g.* the GO 242). Assault gliders have a low load carrying capacity and low landing speed. The DFS 230, for example, carries 10 men and has a landing speed of approximately 35–40 mph. The freight carrying glider has a greater load capacity and a higher landing speed. The GO 242, for example, has a useful load of 2½ tons and a landing speed of approximately 70 mph.

(ii) All ranges quoted in the following tables are "ideal still air," without any allowances.

(iii) The figures for "troops" under "max useful load" indicate fully equipped men, and include the pilot or pilots.

—GLIDERS

Type	Max useful load (a) Freight (lb) (b) Troops	Tug	Cruising speed (a) mph (b) Altitude (feet)	Range (miles)	Remarks
ASSAULT GLIDER DFS 230	(a) 2,800 (b) 10	Ju 52	(a) 100 (b) 3,000	630	No armour plate fitted. MG sometimes fitted externally to fuselage, firing forward. Portable army type wireless may be carried. Glider may be fitted with tail parachute to enable aircraft to make steeper descent and quicker landing.
		He 111	(a) 110 (b) 5,600	1,340	
		Ju 87	(a) 110 (b) 4,500	760	
		Me 110	(a) 110 (b) 5,000	1,420	
		Hs 126	(a) 110 (b) 4,200	430	
FREIGHT CARRYING GLIDERS GO 242	(a) 5,300 (b) 23	Ju 52	(a) 85 (b) 3,100	620	First pilot's seat armoured (8 mm) 8 MG positions provided, but only 4 MGs fitted at any one time. Telephone communication with tug provided. Use of tail parachute, and assisted take-off reported.
		He 111	(a) 149 (b) 5,600	1,030	
		Me 110	(a) 149 (b) 5,000	1,210	
ME 321 (Gigant)	(a) 26,400 (b) 120	Ju 52	(a) 100 (b) 3,000	550	Originally known as the "Merseburg" until German designation established. Pilots housed in armoured box (6–15 mm armour), on top of fuselage. 18 gun positions available, but not all used simultaneously. Full wireless equipment fitted. Nose of fuselage formed of curved doors providing opening 10 ft 8 in high by 9 ft 2 in wide. Main loading space measures 20 ft long by 9 ft 2 in wide by 10 ft 8 in high, capable of holding a 3-ton truck or light tank. Max load reported to be 44,000 lb. Detachable "extra floor" fitted when operating as troop carrier
		He 111	(a) 140 (b) 5,600	980	
		Me 111	(a) 155 (b) 5,000	910	

.—POWERED GLIDERS

Type	Max useful load (a) Freight (lb) (b) Troops	Cruising speed (a) mph (b) Altitude (feet)	Range (miles)	Remarks
GO 244	(a) 4,400 (b) 23	(a) 126 (b) 10,000	330	Powered version of GO 242. Performance based on rating of French Gnome—Rhone engines, with which one sub-type known to be fitted.
ME 323 (Gigant)	(a) 26,400 (b) 120	(a) 159 (b) 13,000	640	This is the ME 321 glider converted. Overload up to 44,000 lb is reported, reducing cruising speed shown to 130 mph and range to 200 miles.

(19124) G.244 15,000 9/43 K.H.K. Gp. 8/7

Printed in the United Kingdom
by Lightning Source UK Ltd.
113566UKS00001BA/250-252